Paganism for Beginners

Understand and Apply the Practice of Nature Based Spirituality

By: Jane Rivers

Table of Contents

CHAPTER ONE
What is Paganism?

What is Paganism?

When you think of Paganism, do you think of women dressed in black robes around a cauldron on a full moon? Do you think of picking up trash, or a green lifestyle? Do you think of a child who passionately tells another child to stop ripping flowers apart because they are harming the earth? These examples are a few of the countless facets of Paganism.

Welcome to your new way of living! Paganism is a new way to see life. It may bring you unique opportunities, healthy friendships, and a deep love for yourself that you never knew existed!

Best of all, you don't need expensive tools or crystals. In fact, you can create your own pagan altar with just your household items! All you need is a willingness to learn, an open mind, and a connection to nature, which we all have already!

What Defines Paganism?

Paganism refers to ancient belief systems practiced by our ancestors long before orthodox religions existed. Our ancestors would sing and dance by the fire, celebrate the changing of the seasons, and enjoy the moon cycles to support self-healing, manifesting, and more!

In a literal sense, the word "pagan" is defined as a "country-dweller." Essentially, a pagan is someone who worships and cares for nature. This dedication can take many forms, such as becoming aware of earth energy, aligning with the divine plan, and divining messages from the weather. Most pagans have a strong love for animals and preserving the earth through ecofriendly practices.

Every world country has some form of Paganism, including Hinduism in India, Druidry in Ireland and the British Isles, and even Shinto in Japan. Western readers might be most familiar with Paganism through Greek and Roman mythology.

Some might say that nature is the pedestal of their pagan practice. Other pagans have a strong connection to bodies of water, such as oceans and lakes, rolling hills topped by a little cottage, or the whispers of the forest. Paganism can include one or more deities, also known as polytheism, such as Epona, the Celtic goddess of horses, Odin, the Norse god of wisdom, and Hestia, the Hellenic goddess of the hearth and home.

The Goddess

No matter which branch or tradition of Paganism you choose, the entire pagan world is connected through their love and dedication to the divine feminine Goddess. There are many different goddesses, and each one is recognized, even though not everyone worships every goddess. One of the many benefits of Paganism is that we celebrate both feminine and masculine energies, and pagans can choose which deities they honor. Just as women have the ability to give birth, the Goddess is the creator of life and the living. Her divine energy radiates and gleams within us all and connects us to one another. While there are Gods and male energies, you will find many pagans tend to worship Mother Earth, or Gaia, as the main creator.

The Elements

Most pagans believe that the elements have some sort of significance in our lives. They correspond as follows:

North (Earth):
The north is the earth and relates to our health, physical well-being, safety of home, and grounding.

East (Air):
The east is the air and relates to our mindset and mentality (not to be confused with psychology).

South (Fire):
The south is the fire element and relates to our desire and willpower. This element can also be used in cleansing rituals to release anything that is holding you back in your practice.

West (Water):
The water element is located to the west. It relates to our emotions, dreams, visions, and intuitive abilities.

Examples of Pagan Tools

There many tools associated with pagan practices that you may see displayed in a pagan shop, at a pagan friend's home, or on your own altar.

Divination Tools:

There are a wide variety of divination tools available, including tarot cards, bones, runes, crystals, crystal balls, and oracle cards! These tools provide insight into how to better the present and can give a glimpse into the future.

Statues:

Pagans may have a statue of an animal spirit guide or deity on their altar. These statues ward off negativity and unwelcome spiritual visitors.

Herbs:

Herbs have a lot of magical properties. They can help with spiritual protection, lift your mood, and develop psychic abilities. For example, Dragon's blood aids in spiritual protection and psychic development, Frankincense encourages grounding, and Lavender relaxes you and promotes sleep.

Smudge Sticks:

These bundles of herbs are used to cleanse the energy of a house, room, or pagan tool. White sage, which reminds some people of cannabis, is extremely popular; it clears and resets all energies of a space or object. Palo Santo, or "holy wood" from South America, removes low vibrational energies from a room or object while retaining the good energies.

Witch's Almanac or Calendar:
While not necessarily pagan, many pagans do use these books to keep up with the magical properties of the day, week, and month.

Athame:
A ritual knife used to cut cords. Never use athames to cut food or physical items. Athames are only for rituals and used to symbolize energy cutting.

Cauldron:
A small kettle used to burn herbs in. May be used for smudging or to aid in casting a spell. Cauldrons can also be used to burn papers in banishing spells and rituals.

Pendulum:
A pendant suspended on a string or chain that comes in metal, wood, or crystal. Pendulums can be used for healing, divination, and spell casting.

Intentions:
Your thoughts are powerful, and a strong intention is necessary to amplify and direct energy in spells, rituals, and self-care routines.

Book of Shadows:
Also known as a Grimoire or BOS, this journal is used for notetaking and recording a pagan's custom spells and rituals. A Book of Shadows can come in many different shapes, sizes, and materials, from paper to moleskin to cowhide leather. Some pagans also

choose to keep a digital Book of Shadows instead of a physical version.

Offering Bowl:
A dedicated vessel for offering food, crystals, and herbs to deities as thanks and praise.

Candles:
This common item is extremely useful for spells, rituals, and healing. Specific colors relate to intentions and desires. For example, red candles relate to love and passion, blue symbolizes communication and relaxation, green corresponds to wealth and prosperity, and purple is associated with divination and psychic abilities. If you don't have the right color for a ritual, white can stand in for any intention.

Bells:
This musical instrument can signify the start and the end of the ceremony or ritual.

Crystals:
These powerful stones come from the earth and can be used for healing, psychic development, meditation, and rituals. Each crystal has its own specific properties. Some of the most popular include Rose Quartz (love, self-love, and de-escalating an argument), Amethyst (psychic development and protection), Carnelian (creativity and sexuality), Labradorite (spell boosting and relaxation), Selenite (cleansing), and Citrine (manifestation, abundance, and energy).

Paganism in Modern Society

Unfortunately, due to centuries of myths of Paganism being "evil and degenerative," most pagan practices and rituals have become secretive and private. Orthodox Christianity in particular sought to destroy Paganism during the Middle Ages in order to convert everyone to Christianity, even though it folded many pagan traditions into their holidays. Therefore, Paganism still holds an important place in modern society, whether most people realize it or not. Modern technology has put some Earth-based pagan practices in danger, but it has also brought pagan communities together. Modern Paganism practices balance in all areas of life and promotes equality for all races and genders. We believe that everyone has a place in life and that all lives are sacred. We are free to indulge in joys, affirmations, and pleasure as long as we are not harming another human or animal. The old superstition that pagans hide from society and practice malevolent rituals is a complete myth.

What Paganism is Not

Now that you have a basic understanding of Paganism and its place in modern society, it's important to understand what Paganism is not:

- Paganism is not a cult. We understand that Paganism might not be for everyone. Therefore, if someone chooses to leave or change faiths, we do not threaten or punish them.
- Paganism is not a weapon. It is never a way to control or harm others. To that end, pagans do not curse and hex one another for leverage. In some pagan

sects, such as Wicca, curses are actually frowned upon or forbidden.
- There is no required Pagan uniform. Stereotypes say that pagans must wear all black, or have pale skin. This is a myth. Paganism does not have a particular look.
- Pagan covens do not lead drug-induced orgies or blood rituals. In fact, most pagan rituals are quiet, peaceful, and personal, involving only nature, crystals, and herbs.
- Paganism is not a social status and does not give you any leverage over anyone else traveling their spiritual journey. Steer clear of anyone who says you must be certified to practice Paganism.
- Black cats are not the only animal ally.
- Not all pagans are witches, and not all witches are pagans. Paganism is any earth-based religion, while a witch is someone who practices ceremonial magic and may or may not be pagan.

Is Paganism for You?

Paganism may or may not be for you. Here are a few ways to know if you've come to the right place:
- You are ready to take accountability for your life.
- You are willing to let go of stigma and see where this path takes you.
- You want to be in control of your own fate.
- You want to help the earth, worship nature, and befriend nature and animal spirits.

If you are ready to see the world in a new way, walk on your own spiritual journey, and find a sacred religion that can be tailored to you, welcome. Turn to the next chapter, and let's get walking.

CHAPTER TWO
The Forest Pagan Branches

In this chapter, you will find different branches or sub-practices of Paganism. There is something for everyone who is embarking on their spiritual journey. While the majority of pagans are polytheistic, you will see that each tradition has its own beliefs and practices for deity worship.

Hellenic Polytheism

Hellenic polytheism is similar to Paganism and is often considered the Greek branch of Paganism. Just as the word "pagan" describes the many pantheons of nature-based religions, Hellenic polytheism is a universal term for the many branches of spiritual practices that honor our Greek ancestors. Many Hellenic polytheistic groups practice ancestral traditions from Ancient Greece.

Hellenismos

The word "Hellenismos" is used to explain the modernized practice of ancient Greek religions. The people who follow this branch of Paganism may call themselves "Hellenes," "Hellenic Reconstructionists," or "Hellenic Pagans." The Hellenismos path began in 351 C.E. when Roman Emperor Julian converted from Christianity to traditional Hellenistic Paganism.

Beliefs

Just as Paganism holds unique views for each practitioner, Hellenic Polytheists have different values and practices. However, most Hellenics find common ground with these beliefs:

- Credible resources and associations
- Reliable writing, from authors such as Homer
- Intuitive and spiritual wisdom through personal experience

Many Hellenes worship the Olympian gods, such as Zeus, Hera, Artemis, Apollo, Demeter, Ares, Hermes, Hades, and Aphrodite. Traditional Hellenic worship rituals may incorporate purification, prayer, ritual sacrifice, hymns, and feasting.

Hellenic Ethics

Wiccans and Pagans typically follow "The Wiccan Rede," which states that whatever you put out into the universe will come back to you threefold. However, some Hellenics follow a different ethical creed with three main principles. The first principle is *Eusebeia*. Eusebeia is the agreement to live a Hellenic life and commit to the gods. The next principle Hellenics live by is *Metriotes*, or living a balanced life. The third principle is *Sophrosune*, or self-mastery. These principles lay the foundation and provide the driving force for most modern Hellenic polytheistic groups.

A Keynote on Hellenic Polytheism

Depending on the person you speak to and their definition of "Paganism," some Hellenics do not like to be called pagans. While Abrahamic faiths consider Hellenics pagans, some Hellenics do not prefer this term, due to others' false assumptions that all pagans are Wiccan and the belief that ancient Greeks would not have used the word.

Hellenics in Modern Day Worship

Hellenics are no longer found only in Greece; you can find Hellenic groups in virtually any part of the world! In North America, one popular group is the Hellenion. Unlike Wicca or other pagan paths which incorporate High Priestesses, Hellenics learn through personal experience with the gods and reliable sources from Ancient Greece.

Hellenic Holidays

Ancient Greeks loved to celebrate, and Hellenic pagans continue this tradition! Throughout the year, Hellenic pagans hold many celebrations to honor the Olympian deities and harvest festivals to celebrate the Earth's natural cycles. Some Hellenics perform private rituals for their personal deities, which often align with particular days of the week. For example, devotees of Aphrodite honor her on Fridays.

Wicca

Wicca is one of the most familiar and misunderstood branches of Paganism. Wicca began long before the Christian era, and some Wiccans believe in a direct line to primeval traditions passed through ancestral bloodlines. Wiccans may practice alone or in a group, or coven. In 1986, Wicca was officially recognized as a religion in the United States.

While there are numerous ways Wiccans embark on their spiritual practice, many Wiccans are bitheistic, meaning they worship both a goddess and a god. Some Wiccans worship deities from other pagan sects, such as Druidry or Hellenic polytheism, and others only worship the Wiccan god and goddess, often known as the Lord and the Lady.

Wiccans celebrate holidays, too, which align with seasonal changes and moon phases in the Wheel of the Year. Rituals are often at the heart of Wiccan festivals, called sabbats: baking bread at Lammas (the beginning of the harvest), dancing around a Maypole for Beltane (the halfway point between spring and summer), or writing a letter to a loved one who has passed for Samhain (known as Halloween to many, this sabbat is the Wiccan New Year, a time that the veil between the living and the divine blur).

Important Wiccans

Margaret Murray

Feminist, Egyptologist, anthropologist, and folklore author Margaret Murray is believed to be one of the first writers of modern Wiccan rituals and practices. She published many books, including a few focusing on British witches in medieval Europe who influenced other curious practitioners to start their own covens. Her 1921 book *The Witch-Cult in Western Europe* provides detailed descriptions for rituals and sparked a renaissance in modern Paganism.

Gerald Gardener

Wicca's name was first born when Gerald Gardener published *Witchcraft Today* in the early 1950s, appearing as "Wica." It wasn't until 1960 that the additional "c" was added. The additional "c" originates from a Scots-English term for "Wise-People."

Gerald Gardener was a traveler who believed in the occult and is often considered the founder of Wicca. He became involved with a coven located in Highcliffe, England in the 1930s, and around 1946, Gardener purchased land in the village of Bricket Wood, with the intention to create a headquarters for his own coven and a base for folklore studies. Gardener's 1949 fantasy novel, *High Magic's Aid,* became one of the first ever standards of Wicca. His *Book of Shadows* is still a trusted source for Wiccan rituals in the modern age. Initiates of Wicca were required to make their own Book of Shadows in the 1940s and 1950s. It is unknown how the title came to be; however, some believe Scottish children's author Helen Douglas Adams influenced the term.

Aleister Crowley

Crowley was a famed occultist and ally of Gardener, whom he met in 1947. From 1914, Crowley had proposed an idea to start a new religion with pagan origins. These inspirations included celebrating seasons and solstices, and other staples that make up nature-based worship today. Crowley's work inspired Gardener's Wiccans' rituals.

Doreen Valiente

Wiccan leader Doreen Valiente met Gardener in 1952. She reached out to him after reading an article in *Illustrated Magazine*, which discussed the reality of covens and rituals. Valiente revised Gardener's *Book of Shadows,* and the new revisions allowed new generations to consume the knowledge in a more accessible and diverse way.

Raymond Buckland

Explorer and Long Island native Raymond Buckland was initiated into Gardener's coven in 1963. Buckland went on and founded the Gardnerian Brentwood Coven, which was the first official Wiccan Coven in the United States. Buckland was a dedicated proponent of American Wicca. In the 1970s, he moved to New Hampshire, where he created Seax-Wica. This sect blended Anglo-Saxon mythology with Wiccan ritual.

Sybil Leek

Leek considered herself a hereditary witch and promoted the Wiccan movement. In the 1940s, she joined the New Forest Coven. Leek brought her practice into numerous covens throughout England until she transferred to Los Angeles.

Alex Sanders

Sanders was catapulted to fame when his story was told in the film and autobiography, *Legend of Witches.* It suggests that his grandmother carried a powerful lineage that traced all the way back to Arthurian legend and even beyond to Atlantis. Sanders created a sect known as "Alexandrian Wicca," which captured younger generations and became a powerful influence in the 1970s.

Laurie Cabot

Laurie Cabot grabbed attention in the United States when she began to teach classes at Salem State College. She also is known for her aid in helping police solve cases. Her store is one of the first occult shops to come to the United States. She also created the beloved Witches Ball. In 1977, Governor Michael Dukakis deemed her the official Witch of Salem. In 1986, she founded the Witches' League of Public Awareness.

Wiccan Beliefs

Just like Paganism, each Wiccan has different beliefs. However, these are similar beliefs that each Wiccan does share:

1. *Harm None, Do What Ye Will*: This belief states that whatever a Wiccan does, whether that be a ritual, a spell, divination, or celebration of any tradition of their choosing, must not harm any living being. This means no verbal, physical, or intention to inflict harm is permitted.
2. *The Rule of Three:* The rule of three states that whatever intention you put out into the world comes back to you three times, whether that intention or energy is good or ill-willed.
3. *Worship of the natural and supernatural worlds:* Wiccans value preserving the earth. They also worship deities such as gods, goddesses, spirits, angels, and faeries.

4. *Mythological Incorporation:* Many Wiccans add mythological pieces to their rituals and practice. Some of these branches include Celtic, British, and Native American mythological stories, to name a few.
5. *Magic:* Wiccans practice forms of magic. Wiccans practice magic to appease a god or goddess or for spiritual growth.
6. *Feminism:* Wiccans do not believe that men have control of a woman or that a woman can control a man. Instead, Wiccans believe that men and women are equals. Wiccans also welcome everyone, no matter your marital status, sexual orientation, race, or background. However, Wiccans also expect any newcomer to have an open mind and respect for Wiccans who are practicing.
7. *Marriage Ceremonies:* Wiccans celebrate marriage, which is usually held at a spiritual church or in nature. Non-Wiccan traditions such as ring exchanging and cake cutting are commonly seen at Wiccan weddings. A unique ceremony that occurs at a Wiccan wedding is the handfasting, where the couple's hands are tied and vows are exchanged in a sacred circle. After the ritual is complete, a reception is held.
8. *Divorce:* Wiccans are not hasty when it comes to marriages not working out. Therefore, most Wiccans are quite understanding and accepting of divorce. A hand parting ceremony may be conducted, which allows peaceful parting to promote closure and peace as the former couple

continues on their journeys without their partners.

9. *Shrines or Altars:* Like many pagans, Wiccans often have shrines in their yard or house. These altars are usually topped with crystals, herbs, and other items to appease their god/goddess, aid in meditation, and support Wiccan rituals. A Wiccan may also include personal items, such as a scarf or even a purse, on their altar. Each Wiccan has a different way of setting up an altar. However, all Wiccans typically will agree that an altar boosts meditation and magical practice.

Wiccan Symbols

There are numerous symbols that you will see in Wiccan rituals, jewelry, and altars. Symbols are used for protection, growth, and healing. They may also be used to represent Wicca in a subliminal way in case certain areas or people are not so welcoming. Keep in mind that you can use any symbol that you feel helps you with your Wiccan practice.

The Elements

Air: In Wicca, the element of air typically represents communication, the breath of life, and wisdom. The symbol for air can be an upright triangle with a line going through it. You can also use a feather or fan to represent air.

Earth: The element of the divine feminine. This element represents the renewal of life, such as that you would see in spring. Symbols that represent the earth element are a upside- down triangle with a line going through it and even green grass. The earth symbol can also assist you with home life, abundance, and strong family bonds.

Fire: The element of fire represents cleansing and connects to the direction of south. Fire is represented by an upright triangle. You can draw flames to represent fire as well. Use the element of fire when you need cleansing in your life, or when you need to cleanse something, whether that be a tool, tarot deck, or a room.

Water: The element of water represents the direction of the west and connects to healing and purification. Symbols that represent water are an upside-down triangle, a body of water, or a chalice with water inside it. Call on the element of water when you want to heal from emotional hardships and disappointments.

Pentacle:
The pentagram is one of the most common symbols people connect to Wicca. Contrary to popular belief, it is not a symbol of evil or devil worship. The pentagram represents the interconnection between the five elements: air, fire, earth, water, and the spirit. The circle going around the upright, five-pointed star represents protection. Use the symbol of the pentacle to guard your home and ward off unwanted visitors.

Red Flags When Looking for a Coven:
SO, you've decided to join a coven! That is exciting and awesome, but please keep these safety tips in mind.

- Covens DO NOT take part in drug or alcohol abuse or wild orgies. If you come across a group that tells you that you must partake in these activities, avoid them. Covens never force anything, especially anything illegal, on their members.
- Covens DO NOT sacrifice animals. Please do not trust any coven that asks you to sacrifice a living being in order to be accepted into their group.
- Covens that try to force inappropriate sexual acts, such as older men on teenagers, is NOT a Wiccan coven, as they are causing harm.
- DO NOT give ANY coven your credit card, social security number, or bank account. Covens that look for these items do not have your best intentions in mind. They are a scam.
- Covens should be warm and welcoming. They should want to get to know you and be open to answering your questions.

Conclusion

Wicca is a misunderstood, often misjudged religion that dates back to pre-Christian times. No matter what you choose to do on your Wiccan Path, be sure not to cause harm to any living being.

Druidry

When you think of Druidry, do you think of the lush green hills of Ireland? Do you imagine bearded men in large tunics and trousers? Do you imagine men in aprons wielding iron-cast items? Contrary to popular belief, modern Druidry does not always fit the stereotypical ideals of what a Druid may be or look like. If you are ready to take a walk on the creative side, tap into healing, and seek spiritual wisdom, let's take a stroll together through the rolling green mists of Druid knowledge.

What is Druidry?

Druidry is a pagan-based religion which seeks the three most important yearnings of humanity: to create, to love, and to seek wisdom. There are three Orders of Druidry which work with these three important aspects of Druidry in order to achieve spiritual enlightenment. The Order of Druids recognize these three aspects as the Sage, the Shaman, and the Singer.

In Druidry, Bardic teachings help us to feed the singer, the writer, or the creative within us. Ovate teachings help to nourish and build the shaman. The Druid teachings help us to tap into the sage, the spiritual knowledge within all of us.

Druidry in Modern Society

Today, Druidry represents itself in society in three ways. The first way is as a language for Welsh, Cornish, and Breton languages. The next way is through brotherly foundations that work together to raise funds for good and important causes. The third way, which we are going to explore in this book, is spiritual enlightenment. Each of these aspects reflect ancient wisdom from the Druids, who were guardians of ancestral magic and wisdom, which influenced people from Ireland to France.

A Brief History of Druidry

History says that by the seventeenth century, Druidry was eradicated and replaced by Christianity. Despite this claim, many British groups were still interested in Druid ideals and practices. In the eighteenth century, they began to revive the ancient path. This history gives light in today's modern era, letting us learn about the practices and teachings of Druidry from long, long ago. Modernized Druidry leans on ancient teachings, folklore, and mythology.

Druid Ethics

While Druidry is not technically a Wiccan tradition, because it allows for both monotheistic and polytheistic worship, Druids do live by codes of ethics:

1. *Responsibility:* Druid ethics state that we must take accountability first for ourselves and then in consort with others so that we can work to better the world with our best selves.
2. *Self-Knowledge:* Druids believe in being honest about who we are and honoring ourselves, including not doing something that wouldn't be true to our nature.
3. *Trust:* Druids are aware of their spiritual journey and trust in themselves and their loved ones.
4. *Integrity:* Druids believe that when we embark on our spiritual journey, it is partly because we are missing something within us. As we grow through meditation and spiritual development, we learn to find a sense of wholeness. When we fill the emptiness with our newfound spiritual bliss, we can act and respond in the physical

realm with the integrity of who we are, not who we're supposed to be. We learn to see the true essence of our very being, and through that we learn how to apply the whole versions of ourselves in our mundane lives to bring the physical and spiritual worlds together as one.

5. *Courage:* To be courageous is a gift; to be foolish is a curse. A person who is fearless can become blind to dangerous situations, but a person who knows how to utilize courage can be powerful both for themselves and society. Being able to accept suffering and even danger in situations with the intent to make the world a better place, not just for our generation but for those to come after us, is the essence of courage. To be able to foresee danger and still have courage to overcome fear for spiritual bliss, health, happiness, and joy is a Druid's virtue.

6. *Environmental Awareness:* All pagans understand that we are connected to nature. Our emotions flow just like the water does in the creeks, lakes, and oceans. Our mental state, mindfulness, and communication with ourselves and each other whoosh like the winds. Like the earth, we are the roots of our being. Therefore, ignoring our physical health will cause issues if we become ignorant and unwilling to care for ourselves just like we would care for the trees and plants. Our spirit will die, just as the environment will, if we don't stay aware of our surroundings. We need to protect the earth, as she has protected us for centuries.

7. *Generosity:* Be willing to give without expecting a return. This creed does not necessarily mean monetary donation. Spending a day at a local animal shelter, giving meals to the homeless, or even letting a stranger in distress share what they are going through are all ways to be generous.

8. *Friendship*: Friends are the essence of life! Druids believe that friendships are important; however, you have to know when to pull away from someone who may not have your best interests in mind. Your friends should be people who you can trust and who will support you every step of your journey.

9. *Honor:* Honor is being able to navigate life with grace. It is being able to live in an honest, meaningful, holistic way without getting wrapped up in drama or energy-draining situations. Honor is the incredible ability to endure the hard times with a gentle focus, knowing that you will get yourself out of murky water without hurting anyone else.

10. *Worthy Living:* Druids know that *everyone* has a meaningful life. That lady who pushed you at the grocery store, the woman who paid for your coffee, the guy who stole your identity: they all have a meaningful life. Often the people who have done ill to you impart strong lessons. Druids do not take away anyone's life.

Druid Beliefs

Druids do not have an orthodox text or official reference book. However, there are some beliefs that all Druids have in common. Druidry is a spiritual path that for some is a religion, but others see it as a way of living.

Monotheistic Druids

A monotheistic druid worships one god or goddess. They may refer to this deity as the as Great Spirit or Spirit. This term helps Druids peel away the gender identity assumptions that are usually associated with orthodox religions.

Polytheistic Druids

Polytheistic Druids may be animists, pantheists, or believe that more than one god and goddess exist. They recognize other deities besides their own. They also have a strong belief that divine beings, no matter what personal name they may identify them with, are found in all living things.

Diversity

Druids welcome and celebrate diverse beliefs. They acknowledge that their spiritual path may be the one for themselves, but others are on their own spiritual journeys. Therefore, Druids do not tell anyone how to live their lives, because the source is guiding them as well.

Nature is Sacred

Nature is a key focus in Druidry. In fact, many Druids believe that the earth and nature hold the energy of their gods, goddesses, and deities. Druids see all creatures as equally sacred; the human race is just one branch of an entire cosmic family. Druids also partake in studying tree and animal lore to learn how to communicate with nature.

Life Beyond Earth

Most Druids believe that there is life after the physical life has ended, often through reincarnation. In between lives, Druids believe that our souls rest in a peaceful spiritual world until we are ready to reincarnate.

Druid Goals

1. *Wisdom*

One goal of Druids to reach enlightenment is wisdom. There are two stories that provide key knowledge. The first story is the Salmon of Wisdom in Ireland, and the second story brings wisdom in the form of three drops of inspiration. Each story teaches that adults pass knowledge down to children, and each tale has specific instructions that must be followed to gain wisdom.

2. *Love*

Druids believe that in order to experience love on many levels, one must experience it at a carnal level.

The first path of love is peace. Most Druids live their lives as peacefully as possible. Since ancient times, rituals have begun by offering peace to deities or people.

The next path of love is nature. Druids believe that we are in control of loving the earth. Therefore, we must work to preserve it, by planting trees, landscaping, picking up litter, or even volunteering to help build a habitat.

The third path of love is justice. Ancient Druids were lawmakers and judges. They often chose punishment in order to heal rather than cause suffering. Druids utilize storytelling to impart the enlightening values of justice.

Druidism also encourages the path of romance. Druids believe that the body and sexuality go hand in hand. They believe in loving relationships between partners and that sexuality is a sacred way to display affection.

3. *Creativity to Reach Enlightenment*
While this varies from Druid to Druid, many do believe in creative forces such as painting, drawing, and writing. Druids believe that this creativity opens a direct channel to the divine. Think of it like a metaphysical phone call!

Applying Druidry to Modern-Day Life
Druids have a unique ability to find the magic in everyday life through ancient teachings. They have a deep respect for all beings in their life, including life partners, friends, parents, and pets.

Druids also believe in a non-violent life. They do not hurt anyone, emotionally, physically, or spiritually, out of spite. Druids believe that we are all intertwined into the web of life. We are all important, and no one is more important than anyone else. Everyone is sacred and essential. Not only does this belief help us be kinder to ourselves and our families, but it also helps us become kinder to nature and society. If you choose to open your eyes, you will see the entire world is one giant connection!

Shamanism

What is Shamanism?

Shamanism is a sacred healing tradition that connects us to nature and creation. Similar to other pagan paths, Shamanism teaches us to be aware of our connection to the Divine and the hidden messages nature wishes to share with us.

The word "shaman" was first born in the Tungus tribe in Siberia. Shaman has become a term to describe spiritual and ceremonial teachers around the world. In modern times, the word Shamanism has been used to describe various new age circles. However, Shamanism had a long path before it became modernized.

History of Shamanism

It is said that Shamanism began 40,000 years ago. A Shaman spends their entire life chasing their soul's purpose. Before someone can call themselves a Shaman, they must undergo years of study and practice. Shamanic rituals and practices have roots worldwide, in locations such as Scandinavia, Siberia, Mongolia, China, Japan, Korea, Australia, Africa, and the Americas.

Depending on the culture, Shaman meant different things. For instance, some cultures selected persons with a physical illness, disability, or strange physical features as Shamans. Borneo tribes would often select intersex people (hermaphrodites) to study for shamanic work.

Some cultures traditionally preferred male healers. However, in other cultures women were often allowed to heal beside male shamans. In *The Woman in the Shaman's Body: Reclaiming the Feminine in Religion and Medicine*, author Barbara Tedlock shows historical evidence of women shamans dating back to the Paleolithic era. In some European tribes, women practiced as equals to male shamans, and in others, they were even selected instead of men. Numerous Norse stories feature women with psychic abilities, referred to as "seeresses" or "volvas," which means "to see." These female seers would often begin with repetitive verbal chanting to reach the gods. In Celtic lore, nine priestesses, who were gifted with the art of prophetic visions, lived on the island of Breton and performed an array of shamanic responsibilities.

In modern times, many pagans participate in shaman-inspired rituals. These modernized practices include communicating with animal spirit guides or totems, dream journeys, visionary missions, trance meditations, and astral traveling. Please bear in mind that modern Shamanism is not the same as Shamanism in ancient times.

Beliefs and Practices

Early Shamanistic beliefs and practices were established as a way to explain life's complexities and control nature. For example, a Shaman may leave an offering to their gods and goddesses so that they can have ideal weather for growing crops. Communities became reliant on Shamans to ensure well-being for all.

Interconnectedness

A common belief among Shamans is that everything is interconnected. All forms of life are sacred and hold a meaningful place on the earth. All beings are sacred, have a soul, and possess a divine connection to the Otherworld. This fact allows Shamans to travel between worlds in order to communicate with spirits, connecting this world and the Otherworld.

Shamans are often relied upon to provide divine information. While these messages are often meant for individuals, many times these psychic insights may also affect communities. In some tribes, elders consult a Shaman before making major decisions. To retrieve these messages, a Shaman may use techniques such as meditation, channeling, and trance to gather information from the spiritual realm.

Shamanic Healing

One of the most vital parts of Shamanism is healing. Shamans are able to heal physical damage created by imbalances or blockages to someone's soul. For total well-being, the physical, emotional, and spiritual selves must be balanced. Shamanic healing is done is through dance, singing, prayer, and energy healing techniques, such as Reiki, where the healer channels universal life force energy into their hands and then transfers it to the patient. Shamans chase malicious spirits from an afflicted person and ensure that they are further protected from any future attacks.

Yoga

At the Chicago World's Fair in 1893, Swami Vivekanada demonstrated India's yoga practice, which uses different poses to improve the body, promote relaxation, induce stronger meditative experiences, and calm the psyche. Yoga can also improve relationships, tackle goals, and heal trauma. Today, Yoga is practiced all around the world, and many utilize the physical, mental, and spiritual benefits of this ancient Indian practice. In Sanskrit, yoga means "to yoke." While many connect yoga to the physical, it is a mindful, soulful practice. Yoga is about doing everything in life with sacred intention!

Soul Healing

Another sacred practice is the act of soul healing or soul retrieval, the process of returning a soul to its body. In modern times, Shamans provide past life regression, where a practitioner will help an individual remove trauma that has been brought into their current life, make peace with their past, and live in the present time.

An Important Note on Shamanism

Shamanism is a rich collection of spiritual practices inspired by ancient shamanic rituals around the world. Modern Shamans have the ability to apply these techniques to their views of life and their place in today's society. Often these Shamans are political activists, especially for animals and the environment.

Asatru: Norse Heathens

You'll find many Pagans and Wiccans today choose to worship and honor their Norse descendants. While many Norse followers use the term "Heathen," you may also hear other Norse followers using the word "Asatru" when they describe their beliefs and practices.

A Brief History on the Asatru Movement

The Revival of Germanic Paganism began in the 1970s, which is also when the Norse movement set sail. It didn't begin truly moving through countries until its liftoff in the country of Iceland on the Summer Equinox of 1972. A year later, the Islenska Asatruarfelagio was officially deemed a religion. Following that, the Asatru Free Assembly (now known as the Asatru Folk Assembly) was born in the United States. The Asatru Alliance, an offspring Norse group founded by Valgard Murray, has a yearly gathering known as "Althing," which has been held for the past 25 years.

Most Asatruar prefer the term "Heathen" over "neo-pagan." Neo-pagan refers to a combination of both new and old Norse ways, whereas Heathen refers to the traditional reconstructionist path that Norse worldwide are working to bring back.

Beliefs of the Norse Heathens

The Asatru believe that the gods are living within all of us and play a role in the world. The Asatru believe in different degrees of deities.

- Aesir Gods: Heads of tribes. They are usually known as the leaders.
- Vanir Gods: While they are a part of the tribes, they are typically consorts. The Vanir gods symbolize the forest and nature.
- Jotnar Gods: These gods are always at war. They bring chaos and destruction.

Asatruar believe that those who die in battle are brought by the goddess Freya to an afterlife called Valhalla. Once there, they feast on a swine who is killed and brought back to life each day by the Norse gods.

A few Asatruar traditions say that being dishonest sends you to Hifhel after death, a place of despair and torment. The rest of the Asatruar are believed to go to an afterlife in Hel, a place of serenity, joy, and rest.

The Nine Noble Virtues

While each sect of Norse Paganism has its own beliefs and practices, nearly all modern Asatruar live by nine modalities known as the "Nine Noble Virtues." This code of ethics comes from various sources. These include ancient historic knowledge as well as literature, including Hávamál, the Poetic and Prose Eddas, and Icelandic sagas.

Courage

Courage isn't just physical energy, it's also mental energy. To some, courage may mean going to war; however, most Asatruar revere emotional and mental acts of courage, defending your beliefs and who you are. At core value, courage is about standing up for yourself and not worrying about others' opinions. It is being able to fight for your beliefs in a respectful, honorable way. If your community shuns your spirituality, you will need all the courage you can muster.

Truth

Norse Heathens believe that there two sorts of truths: earthly and spiritual truth. According to the Hávamál:

"Swear by no path:
But what you mean to abide by:
A Halter awaits the word breaker.
Villainous is the wolf of vows."

The transformational powers of honesty are a reminder to us all that we must speak our truths instead of feeding others lies we believe they wish to hear.

Honor

To the Heathens and Asatruar, honor is the essence of life. This virtue is a reminder to be mindful of the actions we take and the words we speak, because our existence will outlast our physical beings.

Fidelity

Heathens are fiercely loyal. Fidelity means remaining faithful to your deities, family, partner, and communities. This virtue is so important that historical German Pagans automatically shunned any oath breaker. Heathens also believe that if you let down a comrade, family, or gods, it means that you are turning against your whole community and its values.

Discipline

Discipline is the delicate balance between our inner strength and our commitments, making it a difficult virtue to cultivate. Choosing discipline requires quite an extensive amount of dedication and self-control. Discipline is the fine art of relying on your inner wisdom, courage, and commitment to your path, even in difficult times, to achieve personal growth.

Hospitality

For Heathens, hospitality is about treating everyone with respect and being an active participant in your community. Our Norse ancestors believed hospitality was an important act for survival. Whenever someone came to town, they didn't just get a hot meal and a bed; they were protected by their hosts.

Industriousness

The Norse are diligent and dedicated to achieving their goals. They believe that hard work is vital not only to individual lives but also to communities, families, and gods. The Norse believe that we do not have time to sit around and wait for our lives to change or improve. We must make goals and take action toward them, enjoying both our leisure time and our accomplishments.

Self-Reliance

If we cannot take care of ourselves, how can we give our best self to those around us? Self-care is an essential part of Heathenry. Heathens develop a balance between self-reliance and spirituality. This also means taking care of both our physical and mental bodies. Learning to control the way we react to situations, honor our emotions, and make time to relax and clear our minds is an essential part of being an Asatru. When you take good care of yourself, you are also taking care of the community. Health is wealth!

Perseverance

Perseverance is a powerful tool that enables us to move forward on our paths, even in times of chaos and difficulty. Failure is inevitable in life; however, if you can learn to open your mind and look for the lessons, your mistakes are a blessing in disguise. The average person can do the bare minimum and get by, but where is the enlightenment in that? If you want to be the best version of yourself, then you must persevere. Whether you are struggling with career, love, or family, perseverance will help you navigate the murky waters with the light to get you through!

Blot Ritual

Many Norse practice the blot ritual, which is an offering to a deity. It is believed that the word "blot" may have a connection to the word "blood." Do not worry! In modern times, Heathens make offerings of mead, cider, or beer. The beverage is dedicated to the gods and then some is devoured by the Heathen and the rest is for their deities.

Important Norse Holidays

Heathens celebrate four holidays, which are Summer Finding (Spring Equinox), Winter Finding (Fall Equinox), Midsummer (June 21st), and Yule (Winter Solstice). Yule is the most important Norse festival and a twenty-one-day-long celebration.

Heathens of both ancient and modern times believe in nature and gods. They live a peaceful but wholesome life. They believe in truth, honor, courage, and vitality. If you feel a connection to this ancient wisdom, explore further!

CHAPTER THREE
Meet Your Pagan Mothers and Fathers

Meet Your Pagan Gods and Goddesses

Now that you've gotten your feet wet, it's time to go deeper into the pool of sacred knowledge. In this section, you will meet deities from various pagan cultures. You do not have to only follow one pantheon. In fact, many modern pagans are drawn to more than one deity.

How Does One Work with Deities?

There are millions of gods and goddesses. Your chosen pagan path will often be an important factor in who you choose to worship. You may also find yourself drawn to one tradition of goddess and another tradition of gods. You may ask a deity to offer assistance in solving complex problems.

In order to work with deities, first you will need to research them extensively. This step will help you discover appropriate forms of worshipping your deities. While some pagans will argue that there is only one way to honor and work with your chosen deities, that is not always the case. Choose a way to appease your deities that you are comfortable with and that highlights your understanding of them, while also showing them your deepest appreciation and sincerity.

Offerings

Most pagans give offerings to please their gods or goddesses. However, please stay far away from sacrificing a human or animal. Offerings are NOT derived from suffering. Offerings can be drinks, foods, flowers, or stones. Appropriate offerings will depend on your pantheon and deities. Keep in mind, offerings show your deities that you are thankful for their guidance and assistance in your goal or desire. Remember, deities may not grant your wish. You must trust that if your desire or goal is not manifested, your deity has your best interest in mind.

For Deities of Home and Garden

When asking for help from a deity for your home or garden, it is best to give a home-cooked offering.

Food: Breads, grains, cooking oil, salt

Drink: Ciders, milks, wines

Herbs: Rosemary or thyme

For Deities of Love and Intimacy

Looking to bring some love or intimacy into your life? Give your chosen deity of love one of the items listed below, or something that reminds you of romance.

Food: Eggs, honey, apples

Drink: Wine or fruit juice

Herbs: Lavender or sandalwood

For Deities of Gardens and Nature

Gods like Cernunnos already rule all of nature. Get a little creative and try to leave them offerings that they may not have.

Food: Breads, cornmeal, fruit
Drink: Milk or water
Herbs: Bay

For Deities of Abundance and Prosperity
Perhaps you're working on living in a lap of luxury, or maybe you're looking to pay off that student loan or credit card bill. Ask yourself what symbolizes abundance or prosperity.
Food: Grains, cheeses, eggs
Drink: Milk, beer, wine
Herbs: Mint, catnip, pennyroyal

For Ancestral Deities
When working with ancestral deities, you should make an extra effort in researching and creating an offering that they will be pleased with.
Food: Any family meal that your ancestors may have enjoyed as well
Drink: Drinks that may have been passed down through generations

For Childbirth or Fertility Deities
For childbearing or adoption goals, you want to research specific fertility goddesses.
Food: Eggs or baked sweets
Drink: Milk
Herbs: Rose, sandalwood, apple blossoms

Artwork
Many gods adore the arts. You can paint a picture of your god or write a poem, story, or even a novel that shows your respect and honor for your chosen gods.

Furthermore, you can also take a photograph of something you feel your deities would love and display it on your altar. You can also get crafty and create jewelry made of stones and crystals that your deities would adore!

Pagan Prayer

Long ago, our ancestors prayed to the gods and goddesses. Historical records show hieroglyphs that were embellished to worship Egyptian deities. They provide evidence that man's desire and hunger for divine knowledge and connection dates back to ancient times. Divine energy is available to you wherever you are, from China to Italy to Mexico! Prayer is a personalized way to work with your deities. You can shout a prayer from a rooftop, whisper it before bed, or even write it in a journal. You can pray anywhere you choose: a forest, a church, or even a doctor's office. Prayer is a powerful tool that you can bring anywhere.

Celtic Gods and Goddesses

Despite these deities being worshiped in ancient times throughout the British Isles, Celtic gods and goddess still play an important role in many modern pagan practices. Most deities in Celtic folklore were inspired by the different spiritual branches from invaders of the British Isles. Many Celtic writings were destroyed, so most information on Celtic religious traditions comes secondhand from Julius Caesar and Christian monks. Celtic deities are often connected to various labors, such as farming and the elements.

Brighid

Brighid is a Celtic goddess of the Dagda. She is one of the original triple goddesses: Maiden, Mother, Crone. Brighid is connected to divination, prophecies, home, and earth. She is honored at the pagan sabbat Imbolc between February 1st-February 2nd that celebrates the midpoint between the Winter and Spring Solstices. Brighid is the guardian of poets, healers, and musicians. Symbols that may represent Brighid are flames and depictions of family and domestic life.

Cailleach, Ruler of Winter

In various areas of the Celtic world, this dark mother generates winter storms. Cailleach is Gaelic-Scottish for "old woman or veiled one." In tales of Celtic lore, she is the goddess of both destruction and creation. In one story in particular, Cailleach experiences kindness from a man. For his service to her, she turns into an attractive young woman and gives him love and kindness in return. In other legends, Cailleach turns into a large, gray rock and remains in this form until she returns to life at Beltane, or Midsummer.

Cernunnos, God of the Forest

Many modern pagans worship Cernunnos. He is connected with masculine energies as well as fertility, and he is most often celebrated during Beltane, or Midsummer. Beltane corresponds with many animals' mating season and represents lust. Cernunnos is also connected to the forest, earth, and animals, especially those with horns. He is also known as the Green Man for his connection with nature. In some traditions,

Cernunnos is the god of death, who sings to comfort the dying as they journey to the spirit world.

Cerridwen, Guardian of the Cauldron

Cerridwen is a Welsh goddess. She is keeper of the Underworld's cauldron of ancient knowledge and has prophetic powers. Celtic lore often describes Cerridwen as a conduit for transformation. In one story, she chases Gwion, and the two change into various plants and animals. After the birth of Taliesin, Cerridwen throws the newborn into the sea, where he is rescued by Celtic prince Elffin. Stories like these depict change, growth, and rebirth, all of which are controlled by this powerful goddess.

Dagda, Father God of Ireland

Dagda is a god of fertility, prosperity, and knowledge. He plays a vital role in stories about the Irish Invasions, and he is also the leader of the Tuatha De Danann. The name Dagda translates to "the good god." Like Cerridwen, he also had a large cauldron, which is full of limitless foods. Irish folklore says that the ladle is so massive that it could easily fit two men inside it. Dagda is depicted as a thick and well-endowed man, which symbolizes abundance.

Tuatha De Danann

The Tuatha De Danann is a supernatural race said to live in Ireland. These mythological beings have god-like, divine powers. Their skills were derived from the four wise men in the cities of Falias, Gorias, Finias, and Murias.

Herne, God of the Wild Hunt

In British folklore, Herne is the god of hunting and horticulture. He is celebrated during the Autumn Equinox, or Mabon. He is often depicted as a man on a powerful black horse, surrounded by hounds. Herne carries a horn and a wooden bow. Mortals who get in the way of Herne's hunt are swept away and ride with him for eternity. Herne is often seen as bad luck, especially in relation to the royal family.

Lugh, Master of Skills

Celtic god Lugh is worshiped for his gifts as a master craftsman, and he is the god of blacksmiths, artisans, and metal craftsmen. As a god of the harvest, he is especially worshiped during the festival Lughnasadh, also known as Lammas. Lugh is especially connected to creative craftsmanship. He was also a warrior, and his magical spear was said to begin a war.

The Morrighan, Goddess of War and Sovereignty

This Celtic goddess is best known as a war goddess; however, she is also a lady of justice. The Morrighan is often seen as a crow or raven, although other stories describe her as a wolf or cow. These animal associations connect her with fertility and the land.

Rhiannon, The Horse Goddess

In Welsh folklore, Rhiannon is the goddess of horses; however, she is associated with war and royalty. The horse is a symbol of power, and Rhiannon blesses rulers.

Taliesin, Chief of the Bards

Taliesin may be a real Welsh historical figure, but he is also a minor god. Many modern pagans worship him as a great poet. Taliesin appears in many stories from King Arthur to Bran the Blessed.

Aengus

Aengus is Dagda's son and the chief poet of the Tuatha De Danann. He is known for his lyrical and musical talents. Aengus's powerful poetry moved royalty, helped him to win his enemy's land, and wooed the love of his life.

Gwyndion

Gwyndion fab Don is a well-known magician in Mabinogi. He is a counselor and father-figure to his nephew, Lleu. Lleu's magic often helps those around him but carries long-term consequences.

Nuada

Nuada was the first king of the Tuatha De Denann; however, when he lost his hand, he was forced to abdicate. His successor failed, and Nuada reigned anew with a silver hand.

Epona, Goddess of Pack Animals

Epona is a Celtic goddess of horses, oxen, donkeys, and mules, who escorts souls on their final journey. She is also connected to fertility and abundance. Roman invaders even worshiped her in her own temple.

Angus Og, Celtic God of Love and Beauty

To this day, Angus Og's love story is still a popular folk tale. Angus dreamed of a woman named Caer Ibormeith, and he fell in love with her. Angus's mother was heartbroken, watching him search endlessly for his love. After a year of searching, Angus came to a lake called Dragon's Mouth. There, he found Caer Ibormeith in a flock of swans. The swans were all attached in pairs by gold chains: all but one. Angus shapeshifted into a swan and together the two flew far away together. Due to this story, swans are associated with love and eternity in Celtic lore.

Egyptian Deities

The Egyptians had some of the first pagan deities with complex ideals of living. As Egyptian culture evolved throughout the centuries, Egyptian deities did as well.

Anubis, God of Funerals and Embalming

Anubis is depicted as a man with the head of a jackal. He is son of Osiris by Nephthys. Anubis weighs the souls of the dead to ensure they are worthy of being accepted into the Underworld. He is also a guardian for lost souls and children.

Bast, The Feline Goddess

Bast, also known as Bastet, is one of the most well-loved feline gods. In Egypt, cats are often worshiped as deities. Bast is a goddess of intimacy and pregnancy. She is mainly shown as a lioness surrounded by kittens.

Geb, God of the Earth

Geb is the first Egyptian king and the god of the earth. Pictures often illustrate him lying beneath sky goddess, Nut. Geb embodies everything of the earth; plants bloom within him, and the earthquakes are his laughter. Geb guides souls and provides them sustenance as they travel to the afterlife. Geb's name is traditionally chanted to help the sick.

Hathor, Guardian of Women

Hathor is a deity who embodies feminine energy, joy, motherhood, and love. She is also the goddess of the Underworld, and she welcomes the newly departed. Hathor protects women, and she is believed to be present when they put on makeup. She rewards her devotees with fertility, and many of her ritual tools, such as the menat necklace, have sensual connotations.

Isis, The Mother Goddess

Isis is a death goddess and Osiris's lover. When he died, she used magic to resurrect him. Isis is the mother of one of Egypt's most mighty gods, Horus, and the Pharaohs. She is the patron goddess of Egypt as a whole.

Ma'at, The Goddess of Truth and Balance

Ma'at is the Egyptian goddess of honesty and equality. She is the daughter of the sun god, Ra, and the wife of Thoth. Ma'at symbolizes harmony and divine structure. In Egyptian stories, Ma'at gave balance and serenity to the universe at its creation.

Osiris, The King of Egyptian Gods

Osiris is god of the earth and skies, and he is also Isis's lover. Osiris teaches mankind divine secrets. Modern pagans worship him as a god of bounty and the Underworld.

Ra, God of the Sun

Ra was the god of the heavens. He is also the sun bearer, bringing light to the world, and the guardian of the pharaohs. Legends say that he travels to the heavens with his mighty chariot throughout the day. Early texts portrayed Ra as the god of only the midday sun.

Taweret, Guardian of Fertility

Taweret is the Egyptian goddess of childbearing and pregnancy. Initially misrepresented as a demon, she is connected to the hippopotamus. Taweret guards pregnant women and newborn babies as well.

Thoth, God of Magic and Knowledge

Thoth is a communicator for Ra. He is depicted as a man with the head of an ibis bird, wearing a crescent crown to represent his association with the moon. At Thoth's sacred temples, people would often leave offerings of writing cases, inks, palettes, and other creative tools. Thoth assists with magic, writing, and even fate. Some tales explain that Thoth may be Ra's son, but some theories say that Thoth created himself through speaking the magical alphabet. In ancient times he was worshiped at his temple in Khmun. It had later transformed into the capital. In modern times, writing tools along with prayers of healing or meditation can also be used to appease and honor Thoth when asking for assistance in working with him.

Amun, Egyptian God of Air and Sun

Amun was the Egyptian god of the sun and oxygen. He became one of the most significant gods during The Kingdom period, between 1570-1079 BCE. Early pictures of Amun illustrated him as a bearded man with a double plume headdress, but he was depicted later as a man with the head of a ram, or just a ram, to symbolize fertility. His name Amun-Min translates to "unseen" or "mysterious form."

Ba'al, God of Storms

Ba'al is the Phoenician bringer of storms. His name translates to "Lord." He was worshiped in Canaan, Egypt following the later period of the New Kingdom.

Bat, Goddess of Fertility and Success

Bat is an ancient cow goddess symbolic of prosperity and abundance. Bat is one of the most ancient deities, dating back to the Predynastic Period. She is often depicted as a cow or a woman with cow horns and a cow tail. Bat supports a ruler's success, and she allows her devotees to see past and future events. She was consumed by Hathor, who eventually took on her abilities.

Bes, God of Fertility, Sexuality, Humor, and Battle

Bes, also known as Aha or Bisu, is an Egyptian god of creation, sexuality, humor, and war. Bes was also nicknamed "The Dwarf God," and he is one of the more well-known members of the Egyptian pantheon. He protects women and children, battles evil, and defends divine justice. Bes is still worshiped in modern Egypt, and many furniture items are engraved with his image. Bes is often depicted as a bearded, bowlegged dwarf with large ears and genitals, who is protecting others.

Fetket, God of Bartenders

Ra's butler, Fetket, is the modern patron of bartenders.

Hedetet, Goddess of Scorpions

Hedetet rules over scorpions and protects people from their venomous sting.

Heqet, Goddess of Fertility and Childbirth

Heqet is a goddess of fertility and childbearing. She is often illustrated as a frog or a woman with the head of a frog.

Merit, Goddess of Music

Merit represents the divine order and inspiration of music. She structured the cosmos and was the main conductor in the musical songs of creation. Hathor eventually eclipsed Merit and later became associated with the sistrum.

Meskhenet, Goddess of Childbirth

Meskhenet is one of the oldest Egyptian Goddesses of childbirth, and she is said to be present at each birth. She breathes the soul, or Ka, into baby. Meskhenet is also present for the soul's judgement in the afterlife. She is illustrated as a birthing brick, which women would squat on during birth, or as a woman with the birthing brick over her head. Meskhenet was eventually consumed by the seven Hathors; however, modern Egyptians still worship her.

No matter who you may choose as your Egyptian god and goddess, know that you are bonding with a powerful ancient guide.

Greek Deities

A plethora of modern pagans choose to honor the Greek gods, often through Hellenic Paganism. In this section we'll go over some of the better-known deities that the ancient Greeks worshiped, who you may recognize from studying Greek Mythology in middle or high school.

Aphrodite, Goddess of Love

Aphrodite is a Greek goddess of love and romance. She is still honored by many modern pagans who carry on her traditions, particularly by worshipping her on Fridays. Myths describe Aphrodite's creation from white sea foam following the castration of the Greek god Uranus. Later on, Aphrodite married Hephaestus, the warped craftsman of Olympus. Festivals celebrating Aphrodite are known as Aphrodisiacs. While an aphrodisiac was a festival in ancient times, the term has a different meaning in modern society. Aphrodisiacs are known today as foods that put you "in the mood," because of Ancient Roman physician Galen. He wrote that any food that passed gas or created a warm and spicy bite, such as oysters, would increase the libido.

Ares, God of War

Ares was a god of war and child of Zeus and Hera. He became an assistant of justice by intervening in his parents' arguments, and this role extends to battle.

Artemis, The Huntress

The goddess of hunting and the moon, Artemis is still worshiped because of her feminine energy. Artemis is also the goddess of childbearing, and she protects expectant mothers. Numerous groups all around Greece honor her relation to female puberty, childbearing, and motherhood. Artemis is also Apollo's twin sister, and the pair share similar gifts and quick tempers.

Athena, Warrior Goddess

Numerous legendary heroes have received help from the Greek goddess Athena. While Athena is known as a war goddess, she focuses on decision-making to produce a victory, rather than chaos and destruction. She is often referred to as "Athena the Virgin" or "Athena Parthenos."

Eros, God of Passion and Lust

Did you know the term "erotic" is derived from this Greek god's name? Eros is the son of Aphrodite and Ares. Fertility groups usually worship Eros in conjunction with Aphrodite, since he is closely linked to love and lust.

Gaia, Goddess of the Earth

Gaia was the Greek goddess of the Earth and creation, and many modern pagans worship her as Mother Earth. In Greek mythology, Gaia created life from the planets. Her name is also used to describe metaphysical energy that sanctifies certain locations.

Hecate, Goddess of Magic and Sorcery

Hecate's history traces back to the pre-Olympian era. Initially a goddess of childbearing and puberty, Hecate eventually evolved into a goddess of magic and sorcery. She also facilitates communication with ghosts and the spirit world.

Hera, Goddess of Women and Marriage

Hera is the first lady of Greek goddesses. As Zeus's spouse, she is the Queen of the Olympians. While her husband's infidelity may have caused a rift in her marriage, she became the goddess of marriage and sanctuary within one's home. Hera protects women, and her righteous vengeance drives many of the Greek myths and the Trojan war.

Hestia, Guardian of Hearth and Home

Every culture has at least one home goddess, and Ancient Greeks honored Hestia as the goddess who guarded fires and protected the home. She also offers shelter to strangers, and town halls served as a place of honor for her. Hestia's flame is never allowed to go out, and settlers were required to transfer her flame from their old property to the new.

Nemesis, Goddess of Karmic Justice

Nemesis is a Greek goddess of revenge. In particular, she delivers punishments to those who have hurt others. She is a force not to be reckoned with, as she brings divine reckoning for arrogance.

Pan, God of Fertility

Pan is a Greek goat-limbed god. He is associated with the forest and its animals, and he is also connected to sheep and goats.

Priapus, God of Lust and Fertility

Priapus was a Greek sanctuary god. Hera cursed Priapus with ugliness for Aphrodite's connection in the Helen of Troy chaos. Doomed to loneliness, Priapus was sent to earth from Mount Olympus, where he became a protector of rural locations to promote the land's fertility. His statues ward off trespassers.

Norse Gods and Goddesses

Norse and Viking culture worshiped a large selection of gods and goddesses. Heathens, Asatruar, and other Norse and Germanic societies believe that worshipping deities should be consistent, not only during desperate times. There are many deities beloved to Heathens and Norse practitioners.

Balder, God of Light

Balder is the Viking god of light. He is connected to the cycles of life and death. Handsome, vibrant Balder was beloved by all the Norse gods. He was believed to be immortal, but mistletoe ended his mortal life.

Freya, Goddess of Abundance and Fertility

Freya is the Scandinavian goddess of abundance and fertility. Call upon her for childbearing or to gain wealth and prosperity. Freya wears a golden necklace called a Brísingamen, which symbolizes fire and the sun and cries tears of gold. While Freya is widely known for abundance and fertility, she is also a goddess of war, magic, and divination.

Heimdoll, the Guardian of Asgard

Heimdoll is also a god of light, as well as a protector of the Bifrost Bridge between Asgard and Midgard in Norse folklore. He guards the gods, and he sounds a magical horn at Ragnarök, the final god to leave.

Frigg, Goddess of Marriage and Prophecy

Frigg holds potent prophetic gifts and she created divination runes. Some tales describe her as the weaver of the future, and in others, she is the Queen of Heaven. Frigg is Odin's wife, and she was the only Norse goddess permitted to sit beside her spouse. As a mother, she made a pact with poisons, beasts, elements, and weapons to protect her son, but Loki, God of Mischief, broke her trust.

Hel, Goddess of the Underworld

Odin delivered Hel to Helheim and Niflheim to watch over the spirits of the dead, except those who were sent to Valhalla. Hel is responsible for determining the future of the souls who enter her realm.

Loki, The Trickster

Loki is the God of Mischief. According to the Prose Edda, he is "a scam artist or fraud." He is a part of Odin's family, even though he does not appear often in the Eddas. He was known as a troublemaker for the gods, humans, and the Norse men, and has shapeshifting abilities. Because of this negative reputation, he has few devotees.

Njord, God of the Sea

Njord rules the sea and is married to Skadi, Goddess of the Mountains. After being captured by the Vanir, he became a high priest of the mysterious Aesirs.

Odin, Ruler of the Gods

Odin was the king of the gods, and he often went on adventures. He used his shapeshifting gifts to disguise himself. One of his favorite shape shifts was an elder male with one eye. According to the Eddas, the one-eyed wise man brought hope and knowledge. From the saga of the Völsungs to Neil Gaiman's *American Gods*, Odin can be found throughout literature. Legends say that Odin was often escorted by a pack of wolves, ravens, and a horse named Sleipnir.

Thor, God of Storms

Thor and his magical hammer, Mjölnir, have been around for centuries, and some modern Heathens still honor him. Folktales describe Thor as a man with a red beard and red hair. Due to his connection to thunder and lightning, Thor played a vital role in agriculture. When there was a drought, farmers often made an offering to Thor to bring rain to their crops.

Tyr, The Warrior God

Tyr, otherwise known as Tiw, is the god of one-on-one combat, triumph, and victory. Tyr only has one hand, because he was the only god courageous enough to place his hand in the mouth of the mighty wolf, Fenrir.

The Norse gods are full of love, light, and ancient wisdom. The next time you hear a thunderstorm, wave hello at the sky, and the next time you are tricked to trust who betrays your trust, you just might have met Loki. Looking for a long-term relationship? Consult Frigg. Need some help paying for college tuition or a down payment on a new home? Freya may be your Norse goddess! Just remember to honor your Norse god and goddess daily, not just when you need something from them!

CHAPTER FOUR
Pagan Values and Beliefs

Pagan Beliefs

You've learned about the different branches of Paganism and met the deities of many different cultures. Now, we are going to take a deeper look at the core values that many pagans hold dear to themselves and their practices!

Pagans in Modern Day

Today when the term "pagan" is used, it describes someone who worships nature, has a connection to cosmic energies, and honors the changing of the seasons. Many pagans consider themselves a pagan if they are just polytheistic. One of the perks of Paganism is that you can create own your unique blend of spirituality.

It is important to recognize the distinction between the terms Pagan, Wicca, and Witchcraft. Paganism is any nature-based religion that includes polytheistic deity worship. Wicca is a nature-based religion that honors a god and a goddess and has its own rules. Witchcraft is any ceremonial magic.

The Pagan Network

Some pagans practice as part of a network. These groups may be referred to as a coven, a grove, or any other name that the group decides upon. You will discover, however, that most pagans prefer to study in solitude. There is no specific reason why someone may choose a coven or a solitary path in Paganism. Some people have a better time learning and focusing on their own. Others may not like having to abide by a coven or group's particular rules. For other pagans, it is simply because they may live in an area that does not have coven or group options.

The Threefold Law

Many Pagans and Wiccans alike believe in the rule of three. Essentially, this law states that anything you do, whether good or bad, will come back to you threefold.

The threefold law made its first appearance in Gerald Gardener's book, *High Magic Aid*: "Mark well, when thou receivest good, so equally art bound to return good threefold." It has since become one of the core values of modern Paganism. If we surround ourselves with positivity and do good, good comes back to us. If we do bad things to others, bad things come back to us.

Be Willing to Grow and Learn

Change is inevitable. On your pagan path, you will see a lot of changes, from a change of interests to losing friends or even family members who do not serve your greatest good any longer. Some people who once supported you may not support you once you come out Pagan. You must be willing to push through the loneliness and see that your path, while difficult to travel, may be the best you have traveled yet. You must also understand this beautiful spiritual path requires effort. You must be willing to show up and receive knowledge.

Honor Both Your Divine Feminine and Divine Masculine Energies

Most pagans believe in dual energies. In every man, there is female energy, and in every woman, there is masculine energy. Feminine energy is our emotional being, sensuality, and transformative power. Our divine masculine is control and structure. This control comes from leading a life of unconditional love. The divine masculine sees leadership as a balance between mindfulness and emotional order rather than a social status.

Pagans Don't Have a Dress Code

Contrary to Hollywood hype, pagans do not dress in all black. In fact, a pagan can be anyone from a librarian to a fashion designer. While some pagans may choose to wear all black, it is not a requirement. If anyone does try to tell you that you need to look a certain way, please run far, far, away; they are probably not educated pagans. So wear that Juicy Couture velvet sweat suit, sport your Chanel purse, and praise the gods and the goddesses. It is wonderful to be Pagan! Celebrate by rocking your own unique style!

Everyone is Welcome to Honor Their Spiritual Path in Their Own Way

Contrary to what novels and movies portray pagans as, pagans understand that everyone has a different spiritual path. We all practice differently, with different spiritualities and religions. However, everyone is on the same journey to spiritual enlightenment. Pagans do not jam our beliefs down someone's throat. They do not hound someone into practicing Paganism. Nor do they scare them into thinking our way is the only way.

We Are Responsible for Our Happiness and Our Well-Being

Pagans do not look for someone to blame for our problems. As pagans, we know that we are responsible for our life and that every decision we make has a consequence, whether that be good or bad. Pagans try to find the good in every situation. We cannot change how someone treats us, but we can control whether or not we accept their behavior and actions into our life. Pagans know we have the ability to change our lives for the better, if we are willing to improve ourselves.

Nature is Sacred

Nearly every pagan agrees that nature is to be cherished and taken care of. The rock you touch, the grass your bare feet tread on, and the tree you sit under to read a book are all divine connections to the spirit realm. The wind may be your ancestors saying hello. The rain may be the gods sending cleansing energy to the earth. The plants you grow may bring your nourishment from mother nature herself. Many pagans take part in Earth Day, as well as offering community service, such as picking up trash from state forests. Many pagans also believe in replacing what you take from nature. For example, if you pick a bouquet of roses, you may want to grow a rosebush.

Magic

We're not talking about pulling a rabbit from a hat. Magic is an important part of a pagan's craft. Pagans believe that magic has the power to transform a community and foster self-improvement.

Pagans use tools to help them develop their magical craft. Tools enhance the effects and intent of magic, but the most powerful tool is you: your energy and intent. You do not need to blow thousands of dollars on magic tools. In fact, most tools can be found in your home and nature.

You also need to learn what YOUR own meaning of the word "magic" is. You will not find it in a book or a blog. You must discover what your personal meaning of "magic" is on your own. For some, magic is healing and transforming your energetic body to achieve a mission. For others, magic is in the mundane and helps us to see the lessons, even in the darkest of times. Whatever magic may mean to you personally will become an essential part of your craft as a practicing pagan.

Start by practicing magic a little bit. Please do not dabble in hexing or black arts. They are not forces to be toyed with and often lead to far more trouble than they are worth. Which brings us to another important point: no matter what your definition is, whatever magic you put into the world will come back to you threefold.

Pagan Festivals and Etiquette for Attending Them

Pagan Festivals and Events

There are numerous Pagan festivals held throughout the year. Even introverted solitary pagans are known to get out and enjoy the festivals!

Festival Etiquette

- If someone asks for your help, lend a hand. Most Pagan festivals are run by volunteers, and unless they are vendors at the festivals, they often do not get paid, so lending a helping hand can help immeasurably. Even doing something small such as cleaning up plates and food can help the festivals run more smoothly.
- If you sign up for a class, make sure you are ready for it ahead of time. Make sure you have all the supplies you need, and be there on time.
- Be kind to the presenters. Coordinators have paid them a lot of money to come and talk at the festival. They most likely travelled to get there. Don't waste their time. Save the chitchat for after the seminar or class.
- If you have the ability to, consider leaving a donation. Festivals are often done by non-profit groups, and even a couple of dollars helps! Every little bit adds up!
- Going to a multiple day event? Make sure that you pack enough food for yourself. A majority of Pagan events are held at campsites, which means there may not be any food vendors. It's always a

good idea to think ahead and bring extra food and supplies.
- Research the event's policies on nudity. Some Pagan festivals are clothing optional, so you may want to check before taking your kids or family to an event.
- Keep in mind that this festival celebrates everyone's beliefs under similar practices. Your way is not the only way, and everyone is allowed to practice their way. You may also stumble across non-pagans and even Christians. They are welcome, too. A Pagan festival isn't the place to belittle anyone's beliefs just because they are different than yours.
- If you feel drawn to being sexual with someone at a festival, particularly Beltane, please be sensible about it. Always use protection.
- Keep a protective eye on children. Festivals often feature animals or bonfires. It is your responsibility as a parent to keep your children within reach at all times. Festivals typically do not offer daycare.
- Be mindful of whom you are taking photos. If you're in the woods with friends, that is perfectly fine. However, if you are in an area with strangers, please ask them first. Some pagans are in the broom closet, and some pagans may work at a business that monitors their social media presence. Always ask permission first.
- Curious about someone's tarot deck, crystal necklace, or clothes? That's awesome! But always ask first before touching someone's things, especially consecrated items such as

athames, drums, cauldrons, and other items that may have been charged and blessed with energy or an intent.

- Don't haggle with vendors. Most vendors are small businesses, and they work very hard to create their magical items. In fact, most Pagan business owners will tell you that they require equal energy exchange, which means higher prices for their highly developed abilities or products.
- Do not chuck anything into a ritual fire without permission of the event holder. That also goes for trash, any items you want to let go of, or an herb or scent that may cause an allergic reaction. If you feel compelled to toss something into the fire, make sure you check with a fire handler first.
- Be kind to all the workers. As previously discussed, a majority of the workers are not being paid for their time, and they are being generous enough to assist you without compensation.
- If someone seeks privacy or asks to be left alone during the festival, please don't pester them. You may see someone sitting alone at a willow or oak tree. They may be crossed legged, with their eyes closed, breathing deeply. Finding a pagan meditating at a festival is actually quite common. On the flip side, if you see someone crying, allow them to feel their emotions. Many pagans prefer to cry out their issues without someone prying to find out what's bothering them.
- While Hollywood has been known to depict Pagan festivities as drug-induced parties, please do not

show up to a class or public event intoxicated. What you do behind closed doors is entirely up to you. However, you are not entitled to ruin someone's else fun, or even their life, with reckless behavior.
- Personal hygiene is still a thing. Even at a Pagan festival, please be courteous and take a shower before you arrive. Oils and smoky herbs are no substitute for cleanliness. If you are camping out at a festival, please bring toiletries. You don't want to smell like smoke all three days of your festival, do you?

These common-sense tips will help you to have the best time possible at a Pagan festival. Remember to have fun, relax, be mindful of others, and ask permission before touching items, and you will be just fine. Don't forget to say hello to your deities while celebrating!

Pagan Parenting
Thinking about getting your bundle of joy involved in Paganism? Awesome! Getting your child involved early can help them to develop a lifelong spiritual development in Paganism.

Over the years, pagan parents have had difficulty finding activities for their little ones to do that celebrate their spiritual journey. Luckily, parenting is a great way to start showing your kids the ways of Paganism. Your children look up to you as a role model. Therefore, showing your children how you live life as a pagan will ultimately inspire and influence them. Keep this in mind, though, when you are doing spell work. The last thing you want to do is show your child that it's okay to hex or curse others.

Below are ten activities that your child can do starting today!

Make a Wand Together

The next time you are on a walk, have your child look out for a stick that they feel drawn to. Wands help to direct energy into a ceremony or spell. Plus, when your child creates it, it's made with their own energy, which enhances its power. It's best to go with a stick that is about the length of their arm. Check the stick to make sure no animal has formed a nest. Once you bring the stick home, give it a gentle wash with water only. Then let it dry. Once it's ready, you can give your child stickers, ribbons, and even crystals. If they want something attached to the wand, assist them. Once the wand is decorated, you can even hold a consecration ceremony with your child.

Beat the Drums

Drums are part of many rituals and ceremonies. Don't own a drum? You can make one out of a coffee can! Try cannisters of different sizes and shapes and see which ones sound the most intriguing to your child. You can also add other instruments such as a rattle. Fill water bottles with dried beans and shake away! Everyone can join a family band night and raise the vibrations in your home!

Meditation

One of the simplest ways to celebrate Paganism with your child is to practice meditation together. You can begin teaching them to meditate by spending two minutes sitting in the grass and being in nature. Starting meditation at a young age can help your child handle stressful situations into adulthood. You can also sneakily use breathing techniques to help children learn how to count. If your child is older, you can give them ten to fifteen minutes of guided meditation. You might even want to get in the habit of doing it once in the morning, once before bed, or every day at homework time.

A Child's Altar

Your children can also create their own altar and dedicate it to their own gods and goddesses. Have them place favorite items such as sticks, stones, and toys on a small table in their room. Use LED candles in place of real ones if the mood strikes your children and they want to add it their altar. Let them celebrate their deities with their own unique altar.

Get Crafty with the Lunar Cycles

Does your child adore the bright light in the dark night sky? You can have them join in on any moon rituals that you might do. For example, you can make moon cookies to eat during ceremonies. They can also create a moon braid and place it by their window. Why not help them decorate a mirror using lunar symbols? You can also browse the Internet for "moon cycle crafts for children" and see what sparks your interest!

God's Eyes

Similar to the "evil eye" hangings and jewelry, God's eyes are a craft you can do to protect your child. Change the colors so that the energy aligns with seasonal shifts. You can also do them in the color of your family's deities or shield if you have one.

Salty Dough Hangings

Salty dough ornaments are easy and fun crafts. Mix the ingredients, roll the dough out, cut them in different shapes, and bake them. Once they have dried and cooled, you can decorate them with your child. You can google "salty dough recipes" for quick and easy recipes. Some of them even have additional flavorings if you choose to eat them.

Wheel of the Year Diary

One essential part of your child's journey as a pagan is writing down their thoughts and feelings. Take them to the store and have them pick out a diary where they can jot down their thoughts and feelings with each holiday, month, or week. If they are able to use the Internet, have them predict the weather and then include it in the journal. Have them check a week later to see if their predictions were right! You can also have them include other observances on nature's cycle such as when they notice the weather changing, the flowers blooming, etc.

Story Time

Who doesn't love a good story? Set up a circle of blankets around the living room on a cold winter's night, or set aside time during the week where electronics are off and they can sit around for a tale or two about your ancestors!

Sing and Shout and Let it Out!

Along with drums, singing and chanting is another powerful way to raise your vibrations and clear the Throat Chakra. It also is a great way to celebrate the beautiful life of being pagan. You can find a bunch of pagan songs online, or if you or your child are feeling creative, you can also write your own songs. Clap your hands, stomp around, chant loudly, and celebrate with your child! Just make sure you don't disturb the neighbors!

Returning to School as a Pagan Student

For your child, the rising energy of the new school year represents leveling up in education. While this time in your offspring's life can be exciting and uplifting, many children also feel afraid and anxious. In this section, we'll go over easy and simple ways that you can blend your child's spirituality into their schooling so that they can bloom. Having a spiritual routine also can help them navigate change later in life.

A Fun Consecration Ritual for Children

Consecration rituals are great for creating a divine connection to your child's school supplies. Not only does it help them connect better, but it also energizes your child's notebook and pencil to help them focus and better retain information. This consecration can be done at any time; you may want to consider doing it during the full moon.

Items Needed
- Peach, or any fruit you have on hand
- School supplies to be consecrated
- Oreos, or any other baked goods you may have
- Glass of fruit juice

Raise the piece of fruit up to the moonlight or sunlight and say: "Dear powerful fruit, be the symbol of the educator who will perch behind the desk, who will be allowed to feel disappointment if I forget to complete an assignment or I come to class late. I set the intention to have a wonderful connection with my educators for this school year. May they always help me learn and grown with their gentle but powerful wisdom."

Pass the fruit around, and let everyone take one bite. Do not dispose the fruit. Set it aside for now.

Next hold the glass of fruit juice and your chosen baked good in one hand and say: "Powerful (baked good), delightful substance for our tummies, icon of learning and growth, I ask for your assistance to aid the power of this school supply consecration ritual."

Put the fruit juice and baked goods on the coffee table or, preferably, an altar.

Run the writing instruments over the juice and snack and say: "I empower this writing instrument so that I can have flawless writing and grammatical skills whenever I need to write."

Run the calculator over the juice and snack and say: "In the empowerment of the juice and cookies, I ask thee to bless me with the ability to solve math problems both simple and complex."

Now wave a textbook (or favorite reading book) over the juice and snack or cookies and say: "I consecrate this book."

You may continue this consecration ritual for all tools that are needed for your child to have a successful year at school. Once your child's school supplies have been cleansed and consecrated, your child may put their school supplies into their backpack.

Now you will pass the backpack over the juice and cookies, being careful not to spill them. As you do, say this chant:
"School starts soon this year.
I will enter school spreading kindness and cheer.
My school supplies are tucked safely away.
Wonderful school grades will come easily my way.
Honor thy mighty fruit!
Honor thy mighty supplies!
Honor thy mighty snack!"

Now you may pass the plate of snacks and fruit juice around for everyone to enjoy. Hug and celebrate together. You have just prepared both you and your little one for success in the upcoming school year. Can you hear the class bells ringing?

Homeschooling for Pagan Students

If you've second-guessed the public school system or are worried that your child may be overwhelmed by the school's curriculum and environment, you may want to check out homeschooling. There are pros and cons to both homeschooling and traditional school; choose what works best for your family.

Unschooling

One thing that most of the homeschooling community agrees on is unschooling. Unschooling means learning through "natural or experience-based learning." Instead of learning through a book and worksheets, the student is allowed to learn by hands-on experience outside of the classroom. This experience and learning can be done by exploring the natural world.

How to Enroll in Pagan Homeschooling

If you decide to enroll your pagan child in homeschooling, you first need to do some research and see what your state's standards and policies are when it comes to homeschooling your child. See what the local Department of Labor requires.

You may also want to look into joining home school parenting groups to get ideas and network. You may even meet parents that are new to the homeschooling community as well! You may also want to ask your local pagan church or pagan store, or search for Facebook groups.

Don't be afraid to get creative with your lesson plans once you have everything you need to start homeschooling your child. If you open your mind, you can easily find innovative ways to include Paganism in the curriculum. Who knew the gods and goddesses could be such wise and educational leaders?

Homeschooling Sources to Check Out

Pagan Moonbeams Newsletter- This newsletter includes customized ideas to celebrate the sabbats and holidays, and a crossword puzzle. The Pagan Moonbeams take a specific interest in the community, and it's something you don't want to miss out on. Your little ones will love it, and you will have clarity on where to start on pagan homeschooling if you are new to the community.

Little Pagan Acorns- Fun printouts that are designed around the themes of Paganism and homeschooling.

Oak Meadow Homeschool- Although not pagan, they offer customizable homeschooling lesson plans.

Unitarian Universalist Homeschoolers- These lessons plans are ideal for those whose local school organizations require a parent organization and homeschooling host.

Raising a Wiccan or Pagan Young Adult
Being a teenager is tough. Hormones are out of balance. Moods are changing faster than the days of the week. Your teenage daughter tells you she hates her life. For most teenagers, rebelling is a normal part of

growing up. While stretching their boundaries, many teens find Paganism.

Devoted Pagan or Rebellious Youth?
It is important to remember that Paganism in itself is NOT harmful or ill causing. However, you should also note that many teens like the idea of Paganism because it's a way to act out. Some teenagers may choose Paganism as a way of lashing out or trying to get your attention. Slow down and be open to your teenager's needs and choices. As long as they aren't toying with the dark arts or extremely dangerous spells, exploring Paganism as a teenager is completely harmless.

Have a Heart-to-Heart
Even if your teen tries to deny it, this is an especially trying time in their life. Even when they push your buttons, shoo you away, or slam the door in your face, your teenager needs you the most in their life. Especially right now.

One of the best ways to help your child is to have open-ended conversations about their newfound spiritual path. In a nice, calm, and relaxed way, ask them, "What is it about Paganism that attracts you? How do you think this will help you grow in your life?" Asking them open-ended questions not only improves your bond, but it also teaches them to think critically and provide an honest answer.

Incorporating Paganism into Their Everyday Life

You will most likely want to create some boundaries when it comes to allowing your teenager to explore Paganism. Not many parents would want their child to wave around a consecrated wand to look threatening. Not to mention, spell work can be dangerous. Do research and find ways to practice safely, such as using candles responsibly or replacing them with LED candles. You may also want to call a family meeting and explain to others that you are giving permission to your child to study their pagan path.

When it comes down to it, communication, setting boundaries, and preparing less spiritual family members will help you to aid in developing your child's spiritual path as a growing pagan.

CHAPTER FIVE
Pagan Traditions for Momentous Occasions

Pagan Rites of Passage

While pagans mostly celebrate the earth's natural cycles, they also believe in celebrating important parts of a person's life. These rites of passage include birth, coming out, initiation, and death.

It's important to remember that these celebrations should be completely tailored to you and your personal spiritual path. If you want to think outside the box, just go for it! In fact, the more personal a rite of passage is, the stronger the ritual becomes.

What is a Rite of Passage?
A Pagan Rite of Passage is a ritual that honors major stages in life, including birth, a new school, entering puberty, death, entering a new home, or even starting a new career.

Why Should You Have a Rite of Passage?
Not only do Rites of Passage celebrate the big moments in life that help us transform, but they also clear our energy so that we can begin the new phase of our lives.

Ready to celebrate the big changes in life? Turn the page, and let's get started!

Pagan Blessings for Newborns

Bringing home your bundle of joy is just one of the many blessings of this life. In traditions around the world, parents raise their infants to the sky and say, "Welcome to the only thing in my life that is more powerful than you."

Welcoming Ritual for a Newborn Baby or New Child Entering Your Home

In many pagan traditions, it is a common ritual to honor a new baby and introduce them to the gods of the house. When you blend this ceremony, your baby is greeted by both heaven and earth at the same time. If you have an adopted child, this ritual can also be done for them as well; the gods do not discriminate. Some pagans call this tradition "a Wiccaning." If you do not connect with this term, you can call it something else.

You can also choose to have this ceremony joined with or separately from a naming ceremony. You can invite whomever you'd like to experience the ritual with you, or you can keep it private to the household. If the hospital stay has been hectic or too much for you, then it is best to hold the welcoming ritual for only household members. Then, you can invite friends and family at a later date for the naming ritual. You can also incorporate signs and symbols that may represent your baby, such as protective crystals.

If you do decide to celebrate the baby's name as well, you may want to also add in plants and herbs that represent your baby's name.

When you come home, stand outside. Take everybody who is with you and have them hold hands, forming a circle around the person who is holding the child.

In unison, everyone will say:
"To the gods that protect our home, we introduce you to our new child.
May you always watch over him/her/them.
May you always shield her from danger.
May you love her as if she were your own.
This is now her home as well. Please honor her and treat her well."

Pass a glass of water, milk, or juice around. Each person takes a drink from the cup and passes it until the entire circle has had a sip. Now touch the glass gently to the baby or child's lips. Leave some liquid in the glass for later on in the ceremony.

Next say, "May the gods that love and adore us provide you (insert baby's name) with the same love and care they have shown us."

Open the door to your home, so everyone can enter, and gather around your altar. The person holding the baby should stand in the middle, with everyone else forming a circle around them.

You will once again repeat the same chant from before:
"To the gods that protect our home, we introduce you to our new child.

May you always watch over him/her/them.
May you always shield her from danger.
May you love her as if she were your own.
This is now her home as well. Please honor her and treat her well."

Now you pass the beverage again and let everyone take another sip. Make sure to also touch the glass to the baby's mouth. Once everyone has taken a sip, leave it on your altar until the next morning as an offering to your gods and guardians of the home. Then, take the cup outdoors and pour it onto the ground as an offering to the spirits that are watching over the outside of your home.

Baby Naming Celebration

Now that you've had your household blessing for the baby, it's time for the naming celebration, where the baby is officially given their name. Some spiritual paths call this tradition a "saining." No matter what name you give the celebration, it is a way to celebrate your baby with your community. Feel free to customize this ritual any way that you feel fit.

Before the ritual, you will have already picked out the baby's name. If you're looking for a Pagan-specific name, here are a few tips.

Something to Avoid When Choosing a Pagan Name
As "cute" as you may think it is, please refrain from naming your child something that starts with Lord or

Lady. These terms are reserved for someone who has years of experience. For example, you may see a psychic medium who uses the term Lady Aryanna Meade, or a High Priest or High Priestess may use the term Lord or Lady in their Leadership role at their local Pagan Church. In the many branches of Paganism, it is an insult to name yourself after a high standing such as that of a god or goddess.

If you want to name your child after a god or goddess, you may want to alter the first name after your chosen deity. For example, you could call your child "Eponialyn" after the Celtic horse goddess. You may also want to consider meeting your deities in meditation and asking them for permission before you name your child after them. It's not a requirement; however, your god or goddess will appreciate the effort and consideration.

Pagan Baby Naming Method One: Research
One of the simplest ways to discover a name for your baby is research. For example, you may want to honor your Native American heritage, and you also want a name that means wolf. So, you could research "Native American names that mean wolf" and see what comes up and resonates with you. This method can be applied for any tradition or heritage out there, but be sure to avoid cultural appropriation!

Pagan Baby Naming Method Two: Using the Magical Alphabet
Magical alphabets are usually only used in initiation ceremonies and not often used outside of the circle or a

coven. However, there is no crime in using a birth number to find your baby's first name. To find the name, add the birthday in singular numbers. For example, if your birthday is June 12th, 1989 you would add 0+6+0+12+1+9+8+9 to equal 45. Then you add 4+5, which will give you 9, the magical number for your child's first name. If your baby already has a birthday, you can just use their birthday. Now, jumble around names until the number comes out to nine in the magical alphabet:

1= A,J,S
2= B,K,T
3= C,L,U
4= D,M,V
5= E,N,W
6= F,O,X
7= G,P,Y
8= H,Q,Z
9= I,R

When you have a few first names written out, add the letters together using the corresponding numbers. Then if it comes out to a double digit, add it together until it becomes a single digit. If the single digit comes out to your magical birth number or your baby's magical number, then you have found the first name for your baby.

Pagan Baby Naming Method Three:
Dreamscaping With Deities
Another unique way to find your baby's pagan name is to consult with your deities through dreams. Make

sure you have a journal handy, and place it on your nightstand before bedtime. If you have a piece of amethyst and quartz, place them under your pillow. You may want to drink a cup of chamomile tea or do a yoga for bed practice to ensure you are fully relaxed. Once you are ready for sleep, hold the amethyst stone in hand and ask your deities, "What should I name my baby in honor of you?" Close your eyes, lay down, and enter the realm of dreams. When you wake up the next morning, write the answer in your journal. It may take you a few tries to get an answer and remember it in the physical realm. You may also want to make some sort of offering to appease your deities and show your respect for their assistance with naming your baby.

Pagan Baby Naming Method Four: Meditation During Pregnancy

The fourth baby naming method we're going to cover is one that you can do while you are pregnant with you child. When you are able to, find ten minutes and sit quietly. It can be in your backyard, a local park, or a private room. Make sure you are in loose, comfortable clothes. Take five deep breaths, letting your entire body relax. Take this time to allow yourself to just be one with your surroundings. When you are ready, focus on the energy of the baby and ask, "What do you want me to call you?"

When you have the answer, thank the baby for speaking with you. Slowly open your eyes, and then write the names that you heard. It may take a few tries; remember to be patient with yourself. This method also strengthens your bond with your child.

The Importance of Baby Naming Ceremonies

Baby naming ceremonies offer a fun way to introduce your new bundle of joy into this life. They introduce the child to their community and ensure that they have a bright future ahead. You may want to elect Guardians for your child at the naming ceremony, the pagan equivalent of Christian godparents. Whomever you do nominate, make sure they understand it is only a symbolic position.

Do not perform the ceremony while baby still has their umbilical cord, as some pagans believe the child is only their own being when their umbilical cord falls off, and they are no longer attached to the mother.

Items Needed for Baby Naming Ceremony
- Guests from your extended network
- A place to host the ceremony
- A sturdy table or altar
- Milk
- Water in a glass or cup
- Blessing oil or distilled water that has been charged by the full moon

Before you begin the ritual, make sure all of your guests are aware that this ritual is pagan so that they are comfortable with the idea.

For this ritual, the parents are the High Priest and Priestess. It is an opportunity to heighten their connection to their child and swear to always take care of the baby with their best interests in mind.

If the weather is good, hold the ceremony outside. If you are going to rent a venue, check to make sure that you can light a smudge stick or incense during the ritual. Set up the altar before the guests arrive. If you are sensitive to light, ask the guests to put cameras away and leave their devices on silent so that you can focus.

How to Perform the Baby Naming Ritual
Ask all guests to stand before your altar so that they form a circle around whoever is holding the baby and the altar. If you speak to the elements or wish to invoke them for the ritual, do so now.

Next, call upon your deities and spirit guides and ask that they be present for this ceremony. Your chosen Guardians will stand before the mother and father. If the baby is a girl, the father will be the High Priest and leader of the ritual. If the baby is a boy, then the mother will be the High Priestess.

Whoever is the elected leader will begin the ceremony by saying:
"We are here, this present day to bless this beautiful girl/boy.
A new child has become a part of our daily lives.
We are here to announce the name of this beautiful being.
To call a child by its name ignites power in them.
Today we give you, son/daughter, a precious gift.
Child, we welcome you with open arms and open hearts into our world."

Both parents should turn to stand facing the guests and say:

"To be parents is to guide and nurture,

To honor and love,

To help them along their path and teach them to be the best person they can be,

To learn and grow but also to learn and grow with them,

We take the position of teacher and student.

We will protect them and always keep their best interests in mind.

We will laugh and smile at their celebrations and joys.

We will cry and hurt with them at the failures and heartaches.

As parents, we walk beside our children, but we also know when to let go and allow them to walk on their own journey.

This beautiful child is the most precious gift we have ever received.

It is the greatest happiness but also the greatest responsibility that we will have."

The leader will now turn to speak to the Guardians and say:

"You stand here before us for the adoration and love of this child.

Will you identify yourself to the gods so they know who you are?"

The Guardians will then respond:

"I am (name), and I have been nominated as the Guardian of (insert child's name)."

The mother and father of the ceremony will then say:

"Do you understand your role as the Guardian of (insert baby's name)?"

The Guardians will answer:
"It is to honor and cherish,
To grow and teach,
To learn and nurture.
It is to help (insert baby's name) if she ever needs my guidance.
I will be her other parent if she ever beckons me to do so."

Put your child upon the altar. If you fear she may squirm and fall off, you can also have someone support her limbs. The parent will then paint a pentagram using the blessing oil or full moon water. While you do this, say, "May the gods and goddesses of the earth watch over this baby. Keep her safe from danger always. So mote it be."

The person leading the ritual should trace another pentagram on the infant's chest and say:
"You are recognized by us, Mother Earth, and Father Sky as (name).
This is your identity, (insert baby's name), and you are a divine, powerful light.
Walk your path with honor of who you are.
May the gods protect and walk beside you today and each day of your life hereafter."

The mother and father will walk with the baby around the circle. Each guest will take a sip of the cup as they make their way around the circle. You may also pass the baby to each guest and allow them to hug, kiss, or bless the baby.

Once the cup reaches the Guardians of the ceremony, in unison, both will say:
"We welcome you (name) to our lives and our families.
Your parents adore you, and we are thankful they gifted your life.
We ask the deities to watch over you, (name),
Over your family's well-being and home.
We bless your family love and light."

If the parents wish, they may raise the baby to the sky so the gods can look at the bundle of joy, too! Then, the entire group will silently pray for the baby and send positivity to them. Ask that everyone holds onto this intent and energy for a few minutes.

The parents should think about what this chapter of their life means, and what needs to be changed. Reflect on the meaning of the word "parent." You may want to jot these thoughts down in a notebook and revisit them, as this definition changes through the years of parenthood. When you and your guests are done, you may give your farewells to the elements and close the circle however your traditions may see fit.

Pagan Ritual for Declaring the Pagan Self

It may not always be possible to meet with a coven to perform an initiation ritual, or it may not resonate with a solitary practice, but you might still want to dedicate yourself to the gods. In this section, we'll go over a simple self- dedication ritual.

What Should I Include in My Self-Dedication Ritual?

This is your ritual, so don't be afraid to make it unique! Your energy gives it power, so please tailor it to your needs. You also may want to add colors, offerings, and symbols that represent your deities. Some people may wait until they've practiced Paganism for a year and a day, but some pagans do it as soon as they are called to begin their journey.

The best time to perform your self-dedication ritual is the night of the new moon, which represents new beginnings. Once you do this ritual, you are promising the gods and goddesses to completely devote yourself to this path. If you aren't willing to continue learning and practicing Pagan traditions, please do not make a promise you can't keep. The self-dedication ritual increases the bond between you and deities, and if you don't keep up your end of the promise, how can you expect your bond to grow? While you are free to modify this ritual, consider incorporating some formal festivities.

Remember, the ritual below is merely an example. If something doesn't fit with you, feel free to alter it.

You can either memorize your self-dedication ritual or write it in your Book of Shadows.

To begin, please shut off all distractions. Draw up a bath and add Pink Himalayan bath salts to cleanse and energize you. Take twenty minutes just to focus on your intent. Ask your deities to protect you during this time. Reflect on your magical path, your tools, your deities, and your needs to intuitively guide the ritual.

When you drain the bath water, visualize all of the negative energy going down the drain, being reborn as love and light radiating into the Earth and universe.

If you are comfortable, do this ritual naked, or dedicate a specific outfit.

Gather your supplies: blessing oil or moon water, salt, and a white candle.

Place the salt on the floor in front of your altar (or on a towel if you are concerned about your flooring). Step on top of the salt and ignite the white candle. As the flame expands, visualize your goals on your pagan path. Focus on your driving reasons for holding this ceremony.

Face your altar and say: "I, child of the gods, ask for their safe keeping in this ceremony and from this day forward."

Brush a pentagram into your forehead using the oil or water and say, "I open my mind to graciously accept the divine wisdom the gods wish to share with me."

Now touch a drop of the oil on your eyelids, avoiding your eyes. Next, say: "My eyes be blessed so that I can always find my way upon this journey with clear vision. May nothing fool me."

Now, touch the oil to your nose: "I bless my nose so that I can breathe in Divine essence."

Next touch your lips: "I bless my lips so that I speak with kindness and respect."

Then, touch the oil to your heart: "I bless my heart so that I may give and receive infinite love in every form."

Touch the oil to the top of each hand: "I bless my hands, O mighty and powerful gods, so that I can help people mend and assist them if they ever need it."

Touch the outside of your groin area with a splash of oil: "May my womb (or penis) be blessed by the gods so that I may honor the divine gateway of life."

Touch the soles of your feet with the oil: "I bless my feet so the Divine may always walk beside me."

For the final part of the verbal ritual, say, "Tonight, I pledge my dedication to (deity). I choose to walk with them on my pagan journey. I ask you, The Lord and The

Lady, to allow me to grow closer to you. So mote it be."
If you do not connect to specific deities, you can always
use Lady of the Earth and Lord of the Skies, or Mother
Earth and Father Sky.

Take some time after you have given your final
pledge to sit and reflect on this ceremony. Feel the
presence of your deities within and all around you. They
come to you with the gift of knowledge. Be gracious in
accepting their spiritual presents.

CHAPTER SIX
Pagan Magic for Healing

Pagan Magic for Self-Healing

Pagans all around the world have different magical traditions, but almost all pagans agree that magic is real. In this chapter, we'll discuss a few techniques and rituals for self-healing that you can mix and match according to your traditions and intuition.

What is Magic?

Magic is the metaphysical practice of bending energy to enhance a situation's outcome. It uses the properties of a situation, time, or a season to produce results, mainly aimed at helping the practitioner or their community.

Magic comes in many different forms, such as herbs, candles, divination, crystals, and ceremonial magic. Each has its own unique power, but the true power of any spell comes from the spellcaster and their deities if they choose to include them.

White and Black Magic

There are two different branches of spell work: white and black magic. White magic is any spell that has a positive intention without causing harm. Black magic is any ceremony used to cause harm to another person. Black magic also includes any spell that takes away free will, including hexing, drawing specific lovers, or breaking up a marriage. Please refrain from black magic. No matter how badass the spell sounds, it is not worth the karmic backlash that it will generate.

Before you perform any magic, you need to create a clear mind and focused intent. If you enter a spell angry, upset, or fearful, it may not work as you intend. The next thing you need to keep in mind is whether it is worth the consequences, both good and bad. You also will want to make sure you have a quiet space designated for your spell work.

The spells we will be going over in this chapter will help you heal. We often are told to get over a heartbreak, loss, and failure, but we do not let toxic energies such as anger and resentment leave our bodies, which can cause havoc later in life. It might make us shy away from falling in love, give up our dream of opening our own business, or even give up our education. These spells will help you to release pent-up energies so that you can clearly embark on your journey.

An Important Note About Magic
While magic can improve your life in many ways, it is NOT a replacement for professional medical or psychological help. If you are concerned over your physical health or mental well-being, please seek help from a professional.

This book also DOES NOT guarantee the success of a spell. You still need to take accountability for your life, and there are many reasons a spell may not work:

muddled intent, the outcomes not being right for the divine plan, etc.

Also, remember that it is NOT your job to change someone else's life or solve their problems. Everyone has lessons they have to learn in this life, and you could interfere with someone's spiritual growth.

A Pagan's Toolbox

Just as a plumber has a toolbox, a pagan may also possess items to aid their spells. Here are some common tools. If you are drawn to using an item no matter how silly or strange it might be, use it in your ritual. Remember, the most important ingredient in spell work is your personal power.

Altar

Altars are often said to be at the soul of any pagan spell work or ritual. It is a surface where ritual tools are kept and consecrated for ceremonial events. You may keep a temporary altar such as that for specific events, or you may keep an eternal altar that changes with the wheel of the year. It's common for pagan homes to have at least one altar. Decorate your altar in any way that you see fit. Some pagans use their altar to celebrate their ancestors and their traditions, while others may honor their deities or nature. For example, if you wish to invoke the four elements, place a rock in the north to embody Earth, a cauldron or candle in the south for fire, a feather in the east to represent air, and a cup or bottle in the west to symbolize water.

Athame

An athame is a double-bladed ceremonial knife that is never used for physical cutting. Athames can be used in place of a wand. They create protective energy and help cast circles. They can also be used to direct energies. You can make this tool with the items you have at home or purchase one online.

Bells

Bells have been used for centuries to drive away evil spirits and raise vibrations so that the good spirits could watch over them. Some circles may also use a singing bowl.

Besoms

Also known as a broom, besoms are an essential ritual tool. While besoms can keep your ritual area tidy, they can also cleanse negative energies. Brooms are linked to the water element, as they are purifiers. You can buy a besom online, at a local shop, or make one of your own.

Book of Shadows

A Book of Shadows, or BOS for short, is a journal where pagans record personal traditions and beliefs. Some pagans like to think of their Book of Shadows as a personalized Pagan bible. They may include different plants you resonate with, crystals you wish to use, myths and folklore you feel drawn to, and even photos of family that have passed on. Did you pick up a feather or leaf on a walk? Why not include it in your BOS? There is no right or wrong way to create a BOS, so if you feel like adding pink feathers and white pearls, go right ahead! You can use any notebook for a BOS. Pretty journals are mesmerizing, but if you're trying to avoid breaking the bank, a simple notebook will do just fine! If you are looking to create a BOS and are involved in a coven, please ask them first. Some covens have a BOS that they pass down to initiates.

Candles

Candles are a staple of spell work. Some beliefs emphasize making your own candle because it holds your power. Charge your candle with your intent to give more energy to the spell. Candles are closely related to power of the element of fire and can be used to represent gods and goddesses. Some Hoodoo practices keep a candle burning for a certain number of days to assist with a ritual.

Cauldron

Cauldrons are commonly used in Wiccan traditions to blend herbs and potions. In Celtic lore, cauldrons are related to Cerridwen, Goddess of the Underworld, Wisdom, and Knowledge. Cauldrons are also great for kitchen witchery, although you should have separate cauldrons for ritual and cooking.

Cauldrons should be seasoned to prevent rusting or sticking, ensuring long-term use. Some have even said that this process can make a cauldron last a whole lifetime. To begin, heat your oven to 375 degrees Fahrenheit. Apply a thin layer of oil to your cauldron and place it on a sheet pan. Bake the cauldron for an hour and let it cool before using. Once you have seasoned your cauldron, you can just wash it out with hot water.

Crystals

Crystals channel the Earth's power, and each crystal has a different vibration and ability. Start simply by working with your birthstone first. Then, research different crystals and their properties.

Pagan Spells for Healing

Now that you've got a taste of different tools used in pagan spells, it's time to put what you have learned so far into action. In this section, you'll find spells to help heal from things holding you back in life. Please note that spells are NOT intended to treat mental illness or physical health, nor should you ever partake in a ritual with anyone who claims to treat medical issues. These spells are aimed to help you release energy that may be trapped within the energy fields causing a misalignment with your highest self.

How to Know if You May Need Healing

- Lack of trust in yourself
- Lack of self-worth
- Repetitively interacting with toxic people
- Fear of love
- Inability to focus
- Loss of interest in the things you once loved
- Jumping from interest to interest

Spell for Mending a Broken Heart

You think you've found your person, and then, they're gone. This healing spell will help you come to terms with the breakup and move forward. Please remember to be kind to yourself during this time; you deserve it. It is best to perform this ritual during the waning moon, because of its cleansing energy.

Items Needed:
- Rose quartz stone
- White candle
- White piece of paper
- Gold or Silver sharpie
- Willingness to let go of the person
- Athame or Selenite wand

To begin, take a cleansing shower or bath. Visualize all of the toxic energy washing off you, and when you drain the bath, release stress, worry, or fear down the drain. Then, change into loose fitting clothing, or remain naked if you wish. Close your eyes and visualize a mighty, golden shield completely covering your home.

Light a white candle and walk in a clockwise motion until you make a full circle. During the walk, call upon the elements or your spirit guides or deities and ask them to protect you during this spell. Then, say, "I close my circle. Only my spirit guides and the elements may enter."

Take the piece of paper and write: "I release (your ex's name) from my mind so that I may have a clear vision and continue my path of life and love."

Light the paper over a sink or flame-resistant surface. Place the ashes in a Ziploc bag and seal it. Do not toss the bag; you will need it after the spell.

Take your athame. Visualize a thin string connecting you to the person. Hold your athame to the sky and say: "With this athame, I cut the connection between me and this person so that I can move on mentally, physically, and emotionally. I wish (insert person's name here) bright blessings in your journey, and I remove you from my life."

Now, slice the energetic connection with your athame. Close your eyes and feel the energy of your ex being released from your life. Thank them for the lessons they taught you.

Now take your athame and slice the circle, saying, "My circle is open but I and my home are still protected from low vibrational beings."

When you are ready, you may snuff the candle. Some believe that blowing out a candle is offensive. As you develop your practice, decide what resonates with you.

Sweep your ritual area. Smudge or clean it with purified water to clear the energy. Then, take the rose quartz and the bag of ashes and bury them in a backyard or pot of soil. Be sure to cover the area. Finally, take another cleansing bath or shower.

Simple Spell to Go Back to Sleep After Nightmares

Did that nightmare seem way too real and terrifying? Don't worry! This spell will help you fall back to sleep and promote peaceful dreams.

Items Needed
- Amethyst stone or pendulum
- Chamomile Tea
- Hot Water
- Tea Kettle or Microwave

Add some water to a tea kettle and bring to a boil. Place the bag of tea in a cup and pour the hot water into it. Be careful not to burn yourself in the process. Let the tea steep in the cup for about three to five minutes. Then, remove the tea bag.

Take the amethyst stone and wave it over the tea three times while saying:
"Scary dreams have come. Now, go
In the name of (insert your deity's name here).
Scary dreams be replaced with healing dreams to help me let them go.
So mote it be."

Mix in cream and sugar to your liking and drink the chamomile tea. Save a couple of drops to sprinkle on your bed, your sheets, and pillows.

Take the amethyst and hold it in both hands. Visualize a purple shield around you and your bed and say: "This amethyst will protect from unwanted night terrors and bring forth a peaceful night's slumber. Blessed Be." Place the amethyst under your pillow, close your eyes, and allow yourself to fall back asleep.

Healing Spell for Letting Go of Beloved Pets

Pets are family! There is nothing more devastating than losing a pet, but this healing spell will help you release your grief and let them pass over.

Items Needed:
- Photo of pet
- Rose quartz
- White candle
- Pink candle
- Athame
- Dragon's blood or Sage incense or smudge spray.

Take a cleansing bath, allowing yourself to release any stuck energy. When you are ready, you can either do this spell nude or in a designated robe or outfit.

Start the spell by casting a circle clockwise around your altar while saying, "The circle is closed. Only my guardian angels, beloved pet, and spirit guides are allowed inside with me."

Light the pink candle, placing it to the right of your altar while saying, "This pink candle represents my never-ending love for my (insert your pet's name)."

Light the white candle, placing it to the left while saying, "This white candle symbolizes the purity and protection of my pet as they cross over into their next life."

Light your smudge stick. Wave it over your entire body and then your pet's photo. Remember to keep the smudge stick a couple of inches away so nothing burns. While doing so say: "Dear (insert pet's name), I thank you for spending this time with me. I thank you for the laughter, the tears, and the beautiful lessons that I will take with me. I allow you to travel safely into your next life (or Summerland). I will forever keep you in my heart and soul. Be blessed, be free, (insert pet's name). Travel safely."

Hold the rose quartz in your hand, and think of everything you're grateful for about your pet. You can either say it in your mind or out loud. As you do this, visualize the rose quartz filling with all the love and gratitude you wish to give your pet.

When you are ready, snuff out the candles. Then, take your athame and cut the circle open while saying: "The circle is open, and I remain protected."

Place the rose quartz and pet photo somewhere safe. Alternatively, you can place the rose quartz in a spot with your pet's bed or collar to create a shrine of remembrance.

Take all of the time you need to grieve. If you have to cry, then cry to your heart's content. If you need to scream, then scream—just make sure the neighbors don't hear you.

You can also complete the spell by writing in a notebook just for when you want to communicate with your pet.

Let yourself heal and move forward. These spells are just a few of many. Please keep in mind that spells should be personally tailored, and you can replace any chants or tools with something else that you feel more drawn to.

Be blessed on your healing path! So mote it be!

CHAPTER SEVEN
Pagan Magic for Self-Improvement

Introduction to Pagan Magic for Self-Improvement

Spells can improve your life with just a few basic household items. Please keep in mind that no matter how powerful a spell may be, only you can better your life. Self-improvement spells are like taking a vitamin. They can assist you, but you cannot fix your life with spells alone.

Purchased Spells vs. Homemade

If you feel more comfortable doing a spell you buy rather than a ritual you do by yourself, more power to you. One thing that you need to be wary of is the kind of spell and its contents. There are some spells that sound way too good to be true. You also need to look into "reputable sources," such as highly reviewed spiritual shops and pagan stores. Sometimes even the top-notch shops hold dark tricks, so proceed with caution. If a spell seems too good to be true, trust that it is.

Purchasing a spell is nothing to be ashamed of, and it doesn't make you less of a pagan. The one drawback to a purchased spell is that they usually have a set, unchangeable ritual.

Ready to supercharge your life with magic? Let's go!

Self-Improvement Spells for Beginner Pagans

Consecration Spell for Powerful Tools
Consecration spells will add an extra bolt of power to every ritual tool. You can perform this spell on any tool, so long as it is not combustible or sensitive to smoke. This spell works best with the full moon's superpowered energy.

Items Needed:
- A cup of water
- An incense stick or candle
- Lighter
- Athame
- Feather
- A stone or a flower

Before you begin the spell, gather the tools you wish to consecrate. Then, arrange your items to represent the four elements: Place the stone or flower at the north of your altar to represent Earth and growth. Place the candle at the south of your altar to represent fire and power. Place the feather to the east to represent air and energy direction. Place the cup to the west to symbolize water and purification.

To prepare, take a bath or shower to clear the energy you may have absorbed during that day.

Begin your ritual by drawing a circle around the altar using your athame while saying, "I call upon the quarters, my deities, and my spirit guides to protect and guide me during this consecration spell. The circle is closed, only allowing my deities and spirit guides inside with me."

Line up your ritual tools for consecration. You may want an extra towel for the consecrated items so that you do not get confused.

Take the first tool and wave it over the north direction while saying: "I infuse the element of earth in this tool so that it may always nourish my spell work on the physical realm."

Now wave it over the lit candle, being careful not to touch your tool to the flame, and say: "I infuse the element of fire in this tool so that it may always be encompassed by my power."

Next, wave the tool over the feather and say: "I infuse the element of air in this tool, so that it may always cast energy in the direction I seek."

Finally, wave the tool over the cup of water and say: "I infuse the element of water into this tool so that it is purified."

Set the consecrated item aside. Repeat the spell for each item until all tools are consecrated. Then, thank the elements, snuff out the lit candle, and pour the water down a sink. Clean the ritual area and safely store your consecrated items. Remember to thank your deities, open the circle, and if you feel the need, take a cleansing shower.

Bath Spell for Protection
Does a cold draft over your shoulder make you feel as if someone is watching you? Does your home feel unsafe? This simple spell will give you a protective shield.

Items Needed:
- Rose petals
- White candle
- Rose and Clear quartz
- Black Obsidian necklace
- Pink Himalayan bath salt

Draw a bath and gingerly sprinkle the herbs and bath salts into it. Let them dissolve. In the meantime, hang the black obsidian necklace on the doorknob and shut the door so that you will not be disturbed.

Sit in the bathtub, and carefully light the candle. Close your eyes and visualize drawing the herbs' protective energy and surrounding your body.

Carefully wave the candle over the bathtub and say: "I am grounded and protected." Repeat this phrase three times, or as many as you need to feel protected.

When you are ready, you can drain the bath. Reserve 1/4 cup of bath water and sprinkle it outside of your home, so that you share some with the earth as well.

Self-Improvement Spell for Absorbing Knowledge

Do you have an important exam coming up? This simple spell can help! Please note, this spell does not work without your active cooperation, and it does not replace study. You can do this spell at any time; however, it is most effective during the full moon.

Items Needed:
- Orange and yellow candles
- Polished carnelian and quartz crystals
- Palo Santos or Sage smudge stick or spray
- 2 teacups
- Rosemary
- Green tea

First, cleanse your ritual area with your smudge stick or a sage or Palo Santo spray.

Draw your circle around your altar or ritual space while saying: "I close this circle. Only my spirit guides and elements may enter this sacred circle."

Boil water in a tea kettle. Once water is ready, pour it over a cup with rosemary in it. Pour another cup of the boiled water over the green tag bag that you will place in a second teacup.

Place hands above the steamy cup of rosemary while chanting three times: "I channel the energy of rosemary for focus and determination."

Run both the carnelian and quartz crystals over the cups while chanting: "I channel the energy of the quartz and carnelian crystals to help me retain important information and improve my chances of (insert desired academic outcome)."

Light the orange and yellow candles, placing them to your right and left side of the altar, while saying: "I empower my mind to remember important knowledge."

Run the carnelian and quartz stones over the candles, then place them on your forehead. Lay down and absorb the energy from your spell for the next fifteen minutes. Visualize yourself studying and getting better grades. Think of the plethora of knowledge that your mind can retain.

When you are ready, snuff the candle and open your circle counter-clockwise with the athame.

Take a sip of the green tea and offer the rest to nature and your deities. Give thanks to them for helping you with your spell.

Clean up your ritual area.

As an added amplifier, you may want to write down how powerful you feel. What does the limitless energy for retaining knowledge feel like?

A better you is coming! So mote it be!

CHAPTER EIGHT
Divination for Pagans

Introduction to Divination for Pagans

Have you ever been thinking about someone, and suddenly they message you? Have you ever felt something was going to happen, and then it does? Have you ever just intuitively guessed information and ended up being correct? You were divining!

What is Divination?

Divination is the ability to see the future through symbols and psychic insight, and it can be used to assist with spell work and rituals. Everyone can develop their psychic skills. What makes psychic abilities astounding and scarily "spot-on" is unique to everyone. Some people see images, some people hear sounds, and some people feel a presence. Everyone is gifted in a different way.

Divination takes work, especially for beginners. To keep your abilities strong, you have to keep learning and developing. A lot of psychics often compare our sixth sense to muscles; if you don't work out your muscles, they become weak over time. The same notion can be applied to divination. That being said, it is also imperative to be patient with yourself and keep an open mind. Doubt can block psychic information or make it harder to tap into psychic awareness.

A Warning About Divination

While divination is an insightful and powerful tool, visions are subject to current energy. A psychic can only foresee information based on the present time, and no future outcomes are set in stone, because humans have free will. Every choice has consequences. Psychic readings and divination are meant to be a guide, showing which path will best serve you.

You should never use divination in place of medical or legal help. Divination provides insight, but it will not fix all of your problems. If a psychic claims to heal you from disease, please steer clear of them. Psychics cannot cure medical conditions.

In this chapter, you'll find a plethora of different techniques and tools for growing your psychic abilities. Ready to see clearly? Let's get to it!

Say Hello to Claire

You may have heard the term clairsentient, clairaudient, or something of that nature. The "claires" we are talking about here are not your friend; they describe a wide variety of psychic gifts. Then again, your "claire" could be your best friend if you develop your abilities.

Claircognition

Have you ever just had a "gut feeling" about something? Chances are that it's claircognition. Claircognition is knowing something without prior study. For example, you may talk with someone and get a gut feeling that they have a criminal record. Then they explain to you that they are on probation. Or, you may speak to someone and just know that you have met them before.

Claircognition is like downloading a song from iTunes or Google Play. You are drawn to the information, you tap into it, and you receive the song or information, either consciously or subconsciously. As you become more aware of your subconscious, you can tap into the information easier.

Clairvoyance

One of the most well-known psychic abilities is clairvoyance. Clairvoyance is the ability to "see" psychic information. Clairvoyants receive knowledge in flashes of images, similar to a photo or movie. Clairvoyants may also call themselves mediums because of an ability to speak to people or animals who have crossed over. There are also clairvoyants who communicate with your angel and animal spirit guides. Clairvoyance can also be used for past life, or akashic record retrieval. Clairvoyants are able to retrieve these records and tell you about them to help you overcome trauma and understand your soul's purpose in this life.

Clairaudience

Similar to adjusting the radio dial and hearing a song that speaks to you, clairaudients are gifted with the ability to hear psychic information from spiritual guides. For example, a clairaudient may hear wedding bells when she speaks to a couple. This information can symbolize a number of things, such as a future or past life marriage.

Clairsentience

Clairsentience is gaining psychic information through feelings or vibrations, and there are many different types. Some clairsentients may identify as "empath." An empath has the ability to sense others' emotions. Learning and controlling the emotions empaths pick up on takes years of study, so an untrained empath may become physically ill, fatigued, or emotionally distraught quite easily. It's like leaving a light switch on all day, every single day. Eventually, the light bulb will go out, but human beings aren't light bulbs and cannot be replaced.

Types of Empaths

Animal- These empaths are gifted with a connection to animals and can tell when an animal feels sick or unwell.

Plant- Similar to animal empaths, they are able to pick up on the vibrations of a plant. They may even be able to communicate with plants.

Geomantic- Geomantic empaths are in sync with the vibrations of the earth and weather. For example, a geomantic empath may be very bubbly and happy when it is sunny, but if it begins to storm, they may become wary, anxious, or nervous.

Turn the page to meet the plethora of different divination tools there are out there!

The Art of Tarot Reading

You have probably seen tarot decks and tarot readers offering soulmate readings and glimpses into your future. While tarot can certainly tell you what may be coming your way, it is ultimately an intuitive tool that delivers insight and advice. Anyone can learn to read tarot cards and their meanings; however, it takes work and dedication. Learning tarot is like learning a new language. You must first learn the basic meanings, and then as your intuition becomes stronger, you will learn how to communicate with each card. As you continue studying, your Third Eye Chakra, the communication gateway between you and divine, will open and strengthen.

A Brief History of Tarot Decks

For centuries, tarot was a playing card game based on four suits (known as the minor arcana today): wands, swords, cups, and pentacles. Ten years following its initial release, Italian creatives designed additional cards serving as an expansion pack to the card game. These extra cards were so expensive that only noble families could afford them.

In 1781, French Occultist Antoine Court de Gébelin created a set of tarot based on Egyptian mysticism, although he did not provide any credible sources. Jean-Baptiste Alliette released the first official tarot deck in 1791, accompanied by a guidebook that echoed Gébelin's work. The most famous tarot deck was released in 1908, a collaboration by occultist Arthur Waite and artist Pamela Smith known as the Rider Waite Tarot.

A Crash Course in Tarot

Tarot decks typically contain seventy-eight cards and come in a box with a guidebook. There are three different types of cards: twenty-two major arcana, forty minor arcana, and sixteen court cards. The major arcana represents large life lessons, and they are the most iconic tarot cards, like the Empress, the Hermit, and the Sun. The minor arcana represents everyday energies, and the court cards often represent people or awareness. Pages generally correspond to children and teenagers, knights to students and young adults, queens to mature women, and kings to adult men and a level of mastery.

The minor arcana is split into four suits. The cups symbolize emotions and relationships, the wands symbolize energy and motivation, the swords symbolize knowledge and communication, and the pentacles symbolize money, home, and career.

Deciding on a Deck

One of the most exciting parts of tarot is picking out your deck. Some pagans say that you should be gifted a tarot deck, while others say you should buy the one that calls to you.

If you are going to buy your own tarot deck, do some research and find a deck that speaks to you. It may have symbols that represent you, such as angels, or animals, or even cars. You can purchase it in a store, or through online marketplaces like Etsy. The most important thing is finding a deck that you resonate with.

Cleansing a Deck

Whether you are gifted a deck or buy used or new, the first step is cleansing. There are many cleansing techniques:

1. *Crystals-* Place your deck on a Selenite slab or Amethyst or Quartz cluster for twenty-four hours.

2. *Smudging-* You can light incense, Palo Santo, or a bundle of sage and pass each card through the smoke, visualizing them being cleansed of prior energy.

3. *Candlelight-* Light a white candle and pass each card over it, being very careful that the cards do not touch the flame.

4. *Energy Healing (Reiki)-* Start by visualizing a gold shield around you and the deck, 360 degrees. Then, imagine white smoke coming from your hands and transferring to the deck. You can even trace the details of the cards, visualizing the previous energy being cleared.

5. *Sound-* Use a singing bowl made out of stone or metal, and run the mallet around the bowl to produce a ringing sound. This vibration clears the energy of the cards. You can also play any song that raises your vibrations to cleanse your deck.

How to do a Tarot Reading
1. Find a quiet place.
2. Clear your mind. Visualize a white, empty room, or anything that evokes peace. Before you touch the cards, visualize a white light shielding you and the deck from low vibrations.
3. Connect to your deities and spirit guides, asking them for their advice during this time.

4. Focus on your query, and shuffle the deck in your hands. When you feel ready, pull as many cards as your intuition instructs, lying them face down.
5. Slowly turn over each card, carefully examining one at a time. Let the answers come to you. Consult the guidebook that came with your deck if necessary.
6. You may want to journal your questions and answers to improve your skills.
7. Thank your guides and the cards and shuffle them back into the deck.
8. Visualize a shower of white, cleansing light pouring over you, your hands, and the deck.
9. Store the deck and journal and reflect on the advice throughout your day.

Storing a Tarot Deck

Keeping your cards in a safe area where they cannot be touched or harmed is vital to protect their energy. You can simply keep your deck in its original box; just be sure to cleanse it after each use. You can also purchase a silk pouch or scarf for your deck to keep dust and dirt from touching them and add a quartz, citrine, or amethyst stone for cleansing.

Divining with Runes

Most Norse Pagans who practice divination use the Germanic/Scandinavian system known as runes. Runes are pieces of stones, crystals, glass, or wood with the runic alphabet. Each symbol has a meaning. Just like tarot, runes are not meant to predict the future as much as they are a guide for moving forward in life.

History of the Runes

The history of runes is widely debated because few primary sources have been fully examined, despite the plethora of runes that can be found throughout Scandinavia. However, many Norse Pagans and Heathens agree that they were imported by Mediterranean immigrants in the first century CE.

In Norse folklore, the story of the Yggdrasil tree tells the discovery of the runic alphabet:

"None refreshed me ever with food or drink.
I peered right down in the deep;
Crying aloud I lifted the Runes
Then I fell back from thence."

Types of Runes

There are a few different types of runes. One of the more popular sets is the Elder Futhark runes, which consist of the 24 Germanic runic alphabet system. Anglo-Saxon runes have 33 letters. Other variations include Turkish and Hungarian runes, Scandinavian runes, and the Etruscan alphabet. Some pagans read with a subset known as witch's stones, which may have been derived from Germanic and Scandinavian runes.

How to Read Runes

1. Just like tarot, you should have a quiet place to focus on the runic messages. You can also read outside as long as the weather permits.
2. Clear your mind and focus on your question.
3. Reach your hand into the bag of runes and rummage around until you are guided to pull out some stones.

4. Place the runes in front of you and focuses on the symbols, consulting a key if necessary. Let the messages come to you.
5. When you are done, thank your deities and guides, cleanse your stones (see the techniques outlined in the tarot section), and safely store your runes.

For an alternative method, place your runes on a thin white cloth and hold it up to the sky. Then, focus and see what answers come to you.

Buy or Make Your Own Runes?

Consider buying your first set of runes until you understand fully how they work and how to make them. While you are not required to be Norse in order to use or make runes, you should at least understand and try to follow traditional methods. Runes should be made out of stone or wood, preferably from a nut tree. You should also use red paint in order to symbolize blood, the main ingredient of life, and our roots.

Now that you have the basics for two forms of divination, turn the page, and let's talk about developing your psychic abilities!

Developing Your Psychic Abilities

Developing psychic abilities is crucial to using divination tools such as tarot or runes, but it can also help you to better understand tough situations and see the light in dark times. Developing your psychic abilities does not have to be difficult. Eventually, you will be able to pick up psychic messages from anywhere. You'll see messages in the sky, the sun, the wind, the snow, and much more!

An important thing to keep in mind is that your friends, your job, and your life will change as you progress with psychic development. As you raise your vibration, some habits and people may no longer serve your greatest good, but you will also meet other like-minded people who attune to your energy.

Become Open to Messages
One of the easiest ways to achieve psychic development is to attune yourself with your surroundings. Start observing weather patterns and the way people walk. Reflect on past failures to see if you can find messages in things that no longer serve you.

Listen Carefully
Pay very close attention to what people say and don't say. For example, if you ask someone how everything is going, and they respond by only talking about their job, they may be having family troubles.

Trust Your Instincts
One of the most important things we can develop as psychics is listening to our gut. The next time you feel that something isn't as it seems, or you get a good feeling about someone, go with it! Your guides are trying to tell you something, so please listen.

Test Your Abilities
The only way to strengthen and align with your abilities is to test them. The next time your sister says

she's running errands, offer to go with her. Visualize a gold shield around yourself before entering the store. Then as you walk through the store, see what you pick up or sense about people as you walk by. You can also create a set of flash cards with different symbols and flip them over. Allow your Third Eye to reveal the image on the other side for you. You can also try this test with a tarot or oracle card deck as well.

Take a Class

You can take a class in person or online, in the privacy of your own home. If you have people who may not believe in psychic abilities, plug in your headphones. Udemy has a plethora of psychic and divination classes. This is a website that can be launched via computer, tablet, or smart phone, has reasonable prices, and most courses offer a certification.

Networking

Another important part of your psychic development is being around like-minded people. With modern technology, we can connect over long distances. Research divination or psychic groups on social media and see what comes up. Just be sure to read the rules before joining.

Now you are on your way to opening your psychic abilities! You may be the next Sylvia Browne; you never know! Just make sure to take care of yourself and develop your gifts. If you ever feel overwhelmed, take some time away to relax.

CHAPTER NINE
Meditation for Pagans

Meditation for Pagans

You've seen women clad in mystic outfits, sitting against a tree or on top of the mountain, crossed-legged, hands folded together at their hearts with their chin tucked in. Or men who are standing straight, one leg bent at the knee, while their foot rests against the inside of their other thigh. They look peaceful and serene, as if their world only has hope, happiness, and comfort. Rest assured, these people have stresses just like you. However, meditation helps them combat stress, see clearly, and handle tough situations with grace!

What is Meditation?

Meditation is the ability to alter your conscious state of mind to connect to your subconscious. This technique can help you to understand the root of issues, see a light at the end of a dark tunnel, and become more aware of the world around and within you.

The Benefits of Meditation

1. **Reduction in Stress and Anxiety-** In a 2012 study, a Netherland group discovered that not only does meditation promote comfort and relaxation, but it strengthens and affects four parts of the brain: the cingulate (center of wonder and self-discovery), the left hippocampus (source of emotional regularity, learning, and

coordination), the temporoparietal junction (which opens the door to deeper empathy), and the Pons (where neurotransmitters are developed).

2. **Strengthen the Immune System-** In a recent study, people who meditated over eight weeks were found more capable of fighting off the flu and creating antibodies.

3. **Reduce Pain-** A study in 2011 observed daily meditation creates a higher pain threshold.

4. **Increase Your Self-Awareness-** Does the baby crying in the store make you want to yank your hair out? Are you ready to toss your sibling's phone in the toilet after it went off all night? You need to give meditation a try! Meditation has been proven to regulate the emotions.

There are so many types of meditation, so you're bound to find one that will suit your needs. Here are a few:

1. **Active Meditation-** Active meditation is where you do something physical, like kickboxing or walking, and meditate at the same time. Let images come to you, and see what resonates with you in connection to those images.

2. **Crystal Meditation-** Hold a crystal and focus on it for ten to fifteen minutes, letting any image or messages come to you.

3. **Sitting Meditation-** Find a quiet place to sit. Allow yourself to relax and just be for fifteen minutes.

4. **Music Meditation-** Listen to a song that raises your vibrations, and allow your mind to wander with

the beat of the song. This technique can also be great for studying, astral projection, or even pain relief. Binaural beats vibrate at a certain frequency that act as a pain blocker. You can also try a guided mediation, where someone will softly narrate a meditation to help you sleep, relax, or prepare for the day.

You could spend all day discovering the many benefits of meditation! If you're ready to get creative and have more serenity in your life, turn the page, and let's meditate!

Connect to Earth Meditation

Connecting to the earth helps you become more aware of your surroundings, open your third eye, and recharge your battery in nature.

For this meditation, find an outdoor space where you can sit undisturbed for a few minutes. If you are a beginner, start with only three to five minutes and work your way up to an hour. You may also want to keep a meditation journal handy to write down any thoughts or feelings you have or important messages from your spirit guides.

Begin this meditation clad in loose, comfy clothes. You may want to consider doing this meditation first thing in the morning and/or last thing at night. Remember, this is your meditation practice; do what feels right for you.

Sit up straight, or lay down; it does not matter so long as you can feel the earth. Start by taking five deep breaths. Feel the tension releasing from your body. Notice the crisp scent of the leaves, the woodsy scent of the soil, the gentle kiss of the wind against your bare shoulders. Feel the air caress your face and hair as it flows by you.

Now, shift your attention to the loving sun leaving warm kisses on your eyes, nose, cheeks, and lips. Allow that blissful, nurturing feeling to flow through your body. Feel the sun cascading its way down your head, your neck, melting any sorrow encased in your heart. Feel it trail down your powerful core, hips, legs, feet, and toes. Notice the connection between your feet and the earth. Now, visualize the sun's energy radiating into the ground.

Take a few moments to just be. Let any bothersome thoughts drift away with the wind.

When you are ready, take five deep breaths and allow yourself to return to the present, renewed and in sync with nature.

If you received any messages, write them in a journal. Slowly open your eyes and thank your deities and the earth for this beautiful meditation. Get up at a leisurely pace and return to your day.

Meditation to Connect to Your Animal Spirit Guide

This meditation will help you to meet your animal spirit guide. Animal spirit guides are usually not our pets. They are ethereal beings that guide and protect us while allowing us to learn on our own as well. Some animal spirit guides change, and others may stay with us for our whole lives. This meditation will also help you recognize any signs that an animal spirit guide is trying to reach out to you. Often, people discover the animal they fear the most is an animal spirit guide who has a powerful lesson to teach.

For this meditation, all you will need is a quiet place where you can focus for ten minutes. You do not need to be outside for this meditation.

Begin by sitting or lying down, in comfy clothes.

Take five deep breaths, imagining a gold shield covering you 360 degrees. Ask for your spirit guides and deities to protect you during this meditation.

Visualize yourself in a meadow, filled with any colors or plants you desire. Next, see yourself walking through the deep green forest. Feel the cool soil of the forest floor against your bare feet.

You come up to a beautiful pond with fresh water that you can drink. The pond is full of beautiful, floating flowers and lily pads. Kneel at the pond and drink a handful of healing, delicious water. Stare into the pond and ask who your animal spirit guide is. Focus on the water, letting it reflect your animal spirit guide.

You look to your right and see your animal spirit guide standing beside you. You may ask them anything you'd like, especially for any guidance they may have. Take note of all the things they tell you.

Thank them and wave goodbye. Return back to the meadow where you began your meditation.

Take five deep breaths and slowly open your eyes, returning to the present time.

You may want to write down any messages your animal spirit guides give you in a notebook. You'll be surprised to see different signs from them appear during your daily life.

Meditation is something that anyone can do. You can even teach your children to meditate if you wish. Remember to take meditation at your own pace. You do not have to be perfect, nor do you have to do it for a long time. In fact, three to five minutes a day is perfectly fine for beginners. Keep practicing, and soon you'll be meditating for an hour! Just make sure you don't forget to secure your environment beforehand, such as turning off the stove. Fire alarms are not a pleasant way to be brought back to the present.

CHAPTER TEN
Being Pagan in the Closet

Being Pagan in the Closet

One of the most tedious things about being a pagan is that not everyone agrees with your choice, but that's okay! Everyone is entitled to their opinion, but they have to respect your boundaries. You are not obligated to spend time around anyone or attend any event that may make you feel uncomfortable as a pagan. We'll talk about how to deal with being pagan in the closet in this chapter.

When NOT to Express Your Pagan Path

While no one should feel like they have to hide their path as a pagan, unfortunately in some instances you may not have a choice. Some people still believe in stereotypical, fake versions of Paganism. No matter how hard you try, they may not accept you. For example, if you're a full-time writer for an organized religious organization, you may need to practice in silence. Part of being pagan is NOT making anyone feel intimidated and not cramming our beliefs down others' throats.

If you live in an apartment complex, you may want to ask what is okay and not okay to have in the home. For example, some landlords don't allow candles. While a landlord cannot evict you because of your spirituality, they can evict you if you violate your lease.

You can discretely wear pagan jewelry with flower and animal pendants. These symbols also help others feel comfortable around you.

You may also want to download eBooks onto a tablet or smart phone. Then, you can take your practice on the go and study without being obvious.

Create a Pocket Altar

A pocket altar allows you to take your spirituality on the go, providing sustainability and portability. All you need for a pocket altar is an empty mint container, small crystals, and anything else you may feel drawn to add. Tiny doll house items can be lovely additions. Remember, your altar is always most powerful when decorated by you. You can also browse Etsy and check out premade pocket altars for inspiration or to purchase. Just make sure to consecrate your altar before use. You can change your altar to reflect the seasons, holidays, and weather, or your mood.

What Should You Say If Someone Asks About Your Beliefs?

If someone is curious about your beliefs, share away! However, if they are very conservative, you may want to be careful and avoid terms like gods, goddess, triple moon, etc. Sometimes, just saying that you worship nature and practice mindfulness will help someone feel comfortable with your belief system. You may even inspire them to research and practice as well!

The most important thing to remember about being a closet pagan is to be mindful of everyone else, even those who may not agree with our paths.

CHAPTER ELEVEN
Pagan Dating

What person doesn't dream of a life partner?! Before you start dating, it's important to ask yourself what you want in a partner. Knowing what you want in a partner helps you to avoid the people who may not have your best interests in mind. Are you looking for a long-term partner? Do you want children? These are crucial questions that you will want to consider before even creating an online dating profile. The clearer you are about what you want, the more likely you are to find it.

Are You Ready for Love?
Break-ups suck, but if you are holding resentment toward a past lover, you cannot truly love someone else right now. You must learn to let go of the past, forgive your exes, thank them for the time they gave to you, and live in the now. Learning to fully love yourself can also help you love someone else and attract the right partners.

Pagan Dating Online

Dating in the real world is hard enough, let alone for pagans, and online dating can be particularly rough. Here are a few tips to keep in mind:
- Meet in a public place and let a friend know when you expect to be home.

- NEVER ignore your intuition. If something doesn't feel right, DON'T meet or communicate with them.
- Do you want to date a pagan, or just someone who is spiritually open? Not everyone will have their spiritual preference on their profiles, especially pagans. Keep an eye out for language about worshipping nature. If you only want to date pagans, make sure that is clear on your profile.
- Take it slowly, and don't expect to find love overnight.
- Be very aware of how someone speaks about themselves and their views on love. You'll be very surprised what you pick up on when you tune in and let your intuition take over.
- Don't change for anyone. It's cliché, but your person will love you for who you are and not want you to change.
- Be careful who you fall for. Always be aware of who they really are and how they treat you and everyone else in their lives.

Are There Any Pagan Dating Websites?

There are pagans on dating websites, but some pagan matchmaking sites are just scams looking for your money. Here are a few legit, free options:

OkCupid- While not directly a pagan dating website, there are a lot of pagans on there. You can create your profile, browse members, and talk with matches for free.

Spiritual Singles- This dating website focuses on spiritually conscious people. You can browse matches and message your matches with an introduction template. If you want to send the first customized message, however, you do need to pay.

MeetUp- This app helps you find local and online groups. Search "Pagan" or "Spiritual" and see what groups come up. While this app isn't directly dating-based, you can meet new people and build a connection that can lead to more.

Facebook Groups- Head over to Facebook and look up "Pagan," "Druid," etc. You will see a plethora of groups. There are some even aimed around pagan dating; just make sure that the other group members are age appropriate.

Handfasting

If you and your fiancé want to take things to the next step, a pagan handfasting ceremony often accompanies the wedding. Handfasting comprises two ceremonies: the first ceremony only lasts a year and a day. When the couple surpasses this time frame, they will then decide whether to commit as lifetime partners or go their separate ways with a hand parting.

During pagan handfasting, knots are tied around the partners' hands. This tie represents being bound for life. Each partner chooses a color to represent themselves, and the mother of the bride may also add a silver or gold tie to symbolize knowledge.

Some pagan weddings use the African American tradition of jumping the broom, where the couple jumps over a broomstick to symbolize their official marriage and sexual connection.

Should you decide to have a handfasting or pagan themed wedding, please let all guests know in advance, as some people may not feel comfortable. If that occurs, please do not feel like this is a personal attack; it is usually religious, rather than an insult directed at you. You can also subtly combine pagan rituals with more common wedding traditions to create a blended ceremony.

CHAPTER TWELVE
Pagan Self-Care

Pagan Self-Care

The self-care movement is everywhere on social media these days. It isn't just for influencers; self-care is important for all, especially if you are a pagan who does a lot of spell work and spiritual work. Even if you are a pagan who lives a relatively muggle life, you still need to take time for you.

What is Self-Care?
Self-care is a ritual that helps you to feel better and recharge your energy. There is no right or wrong way to do a self-care routine, as long as it works for you and you feel rejuvenated afterward.

The best thing is that self-care routines don't have to be extreme or long. In fact, you only need five to ten minutes. However, if you can take longer, treat yourself!

Lounging
While not necessarily pagan, sometimes we all need to take a breather and just relax. Grab a blanket, tea, and tablet and have at a day of binge-watching your favorite movies or TV shows. Or you can play video games or read a good book. To take your lounging to the next level, set up a fort and decorate it. Snacks and books, anyone?

Cleansing Shower Meditation

Had a long week? Try a cleansing shower meditation. Stand or sit in the shower and allow the steam and water to cleanse yourself of all of the residual energy you may have absorbed during the week.

Electronic Detox

Feeling off after using your phone too much? You aren't alone! Too much time around electric devices can actually drain your energy and strain your eyes. If you feel the need to carry your phone around like a safety blanket, you may need an electronic detox.

Set an hour or even an entire day to stay off your devices. This will not only help you to detox from the electrical currents but also attune you to the world around you, including family and friends. Just be sure you let your boss and anyone else who may contact you know that you are going off the grid for a while.

Smudging

One of the simplest ways to care for yourself is smudging your room, divination tools, and ritual tools. Just remember to open the windows so that the stuck energy goes out the windows instead of staying in your home. You can also carefully run the smudge stick over yourself and allow the smoke to clean your energy fields.

Journaling

Writing in a journal can be extremely crucial to your self-care. It's a safe and healthy way to put your thoughts down on paper. Write about your week or your feelings. If you feel stuck, there are tons of self-care journal prompts online.

Self-care routines for pagans come in many shapes and sizes. What's important is to tailor your self-care routine to your needs. Self-care helps you to build confidence, accomplish your goals, and heal when life gives you lemons.

Conclusion

Congratulations! You now are equipped with the knowledge and skills to become a successful, practicing pagan! Beginning a new path in life can be extremely exciting. Whether your spiritual path takes you down the road of Wicca, or Druid, if you call yourself a witch or seeker, there are countless tools to help you stay your course, and most importantly, stay close to who you truly are.

If you stick with the tools and advice given in this book, such as cleansing yourself and your tools, using caution when setting an intention, being specific about your intention, and not harming any others, you will feel fulfilled and be able to enjoy the pagan lifestyle.

Remember, only you can choose what works for you. If something or someone does not resonate, perhaps it'd be best to avoid them. If you ever feel pressured, definitely steer clear. There is no right and wrong way to practice! You may use what's written here word for word, and you can modify a spell that fits better, or create your own altogether.

This is a path that is dedicated to personal growth. When you're outside honoring nature, doing spell work, or just connecting to your own self, there will always be personal benefit. If a challenge arises, or you begin to feel frustrated that something isn't working as you anticipated, have patience, and trust the process; there is much to learn!

To all who choose to walk on this unique path, enjoy and blessed be!

www.ingramcontent.com/pod-product-compliance
Lightning Source LLC
Chambersburg PA
CBHW061734050726
47598CB00002B/482